THE ARLOO ESSAY MATRIX

A Simple Guide to College Essay Writing

by

Johnson Arloo

For workshops/ lectures, contact:

Telephone: (256) 797 7665

Email: bondukuarloo@yahoo.com

To my wonderful wife, Priscilla, who has been my bedrock.

And to my children, Bryce, Linda, and Avo, who are carving their own paths in this wonderful world.

And also to my late mother, Theresa Edwa Buah Arloo, who did so much for so many people, and my late father, John Benjamin Arloo, who would have been so proud of this book.

SPECIAL THANKS

To all the teachers and professors who have taught and encouraged me throughout my academic career. The list is long but I am especially grateful to Dr. Aloysius Denkabe (University of Ghana, Legon) and Dr. Everton McIntosh (Alabama A & M University, Huntsville, Alabama) for their guidance and warmth.

And of course, to Dr. Rhonda Sherrod (formerly of Alabama A & M University) who reminded me I was an eagle feeding among the chickens.

I am also grateful to my spiritual mentor, Mr. Harrison Nurse and his wife, Ann, for their guidance and support.

CONTENTS

INTRODUCTION

Nothing gives me more pleasure than the look of comprehension that crosses a student's face when a writing problem is solved. And it was in one of such moments that the idea for this book was born.

I had been explaining the structure of the standard paragraph to a graduate student at the Alabama A & M University Writing Center in Huntsville when I saw that familiar look of understanding creep into her eyes. "Wow!" she beamed. "I wish I had had this tool in my undergraduate class!"

The purpose of writing this book is to demystify the essay writing process for students by cutting through the verbiage of textbook material to the bare essentials. In other words, I want to reduce essay writing to its most basic principles so that the underlying logic can be applied across all types of essays or writing. In short, my intention is to reduce the process to its simplest terms—like a mathematical formula, if you wish—so that every student (or people who just want to write for fun) can do so without breaking a sweat.

Too often, I have met students like you who had all the ideas for a beautiful, thought-provoking essay. Sadly, most of them felt inadequate because, instead of going ahead with the actual writing, they focused on the little things that could go wrong, causing them to lose steam. It's like worrying about the Grammys before the hit song is written—you will be paralyzed with fear.

The aim of this short book is to remove this fear and teach you how to write good essays in an effortless manner. It is a self-help book on how to flesh out the beautiful outline on that plain sheet of paper or the computer screen. And then, having honed your craft, you can turn your attention to the other details like grammar, usage, tenses, rhetoric, and the like, which could be done with the help of your English course professors and good language textbooks.

One book whose impact on my writing has been immeasurable is William Zinsser's *On Writing Well*. He mentions in his Introduction that he did not want his book to be about admonitions—"Don't do this," "Don't do that …" and so on. What he set out to do in his book was to teach "how to write about people and places, science and technology, history and medicine, business and education, sports and the arts and everything else under the sun that's waiting to be written about."

I want this book to be a primer for Zinsser's book. I want to teach you the basic processes of stringing sentences together to build your paragraphs, which form the bases of every essay, article or piece of writing "under the sun." After mastering paragraph writing, we will tackle the craft of writing the multi-paragraph essays required in college academic work.

When I was writing this book, the people I had in mind were college freshmen since they formed the bulk of the students at the Writing Center. I have also worked with graduate students. Then I discovered the book's principles can be applied across the academic spectrum—from elementary school to the University. I have chosen, however, to focus on college students. Still, I hope everybody who loves writing will find it useful, whether he or she is using it for academic, instructional, ministerial, entertainment, or other purposes.

Another problem I had to grapple with was the size and scope of the book. Essay writing is a very broad subject spanning a wide range of types: argumentative, narrative, descriptive, process, expository and so on. But I realized that most of these can be reduced to two types: the standard essay and the narrative. When you master these two, you can apply the principles across the other types.

Ultimately, this book is neither a grand effort to turn college essay-writing principles on their heads nor an attempt to reinvent the wheel—it is just intended to make the wheel run faster and more efficiently. This book simply equips you with the Arloo Essay Matrix®, a tool that helps you to begin writing automatically without agonizing about the rhetoric. It is my hope that by the time you finish reading this book and applying the principles it teaches, you could very well be writing essays with your eyes closed, so to speak.

Benny Waddle, a very good friend of mine, once told me: "Nobody is safe." What he meant was that we are in a constantly shifting world, a world where careers turn on the whims of a technological advance and lay-offs hinge on the next stock market downturn. One thing that will never change, however, is written communication. It is the fuel on which modern communication runs. And good writing is the same whether you use a pencil or an iPad to record it. If you are good at it, there is no telling where it will take you, especially in this social media era. But, regardless of what career choice you make, you will probably do some writing. Whether it is a report, summary of a meeting or internal memo at the workplace, or a scientific paper delivered at an international conference, you will need some writing skills.

And you had better be prepared when that moment comes.

Thank you.
Johnson Arloo

PART 1: THE STANDARD ESSAY

CHAPTER 1

COLLEGE ESSAY COURSES – A FRESH APPROACH

I have found that a lot of students have problems with college essay writing. And while we are quick to point fingers, what we need to accept is that it is a problem that needs to be—and can be—solved.

One of the major problems with the standard essay course is that there is too much material. Much of it is excellent material, but when you are struggling with essay writing, those thick volumes of essay textbooks can be very intimidating. I have seen essay writing books with more pages than a Robert Ludlum novel. These scare some of you and turn an otherwise exciting adventure into a chore. As a result, you shut down even before lectures begin.

In addition, most essay courses begin with a lecture on the rhetorics of writing. The instructor tries to explain the differences between topic and subject matter, topping it with point of view, tone, writing voice and the like. A lot of students do not have a problem with that. In my experience, however, the challenged student panics at the mention of such lofty concepts. These words conjure images of massive academic volumes in the vast halls of the Library of Congress. But essay writing need not be a scary experience.

Moreover, most textbooks or courses on essay writing teach that in order to write a good paragraph, you should write the topic sentence and support it with details that convince the reader that the topic sentence is making a valid point. They go on to tell you the paragraph should have unity, coherence, and follow a certain pattern of development while clearly supporting the essay's thesis statement.

This is all well and good. It takes time for students to grasp this technique, but some eventually do. As a matter of fact, some great essays have come out of this approach.

The problem with this line of instruction is that the college freshman trying to create a decent, effective paragraph does not know exactly how much detail should be provided to support his topic sentence. This leads to run-ons and, eventually, confusion: the student strings together a whole series of sentences with neither substance nor focus.

Other teachers describe a paragraph's elements as having a topic sentence, an "order of importance," and a "closing sentence." The problem with this approach is similar to the one outlined earlier in the previous paragraph: it leads to run-ons because the student is confused about "order of importance." It may well work in a classification or narrative essay. But what happens when the student is writing a standard academic essay? What determines that one fact, detail or argument is more important than the other? And what's a "closing sentence"?

THE STRUCTURED PARAGRAPH APPROACH

For me, a better approach to teaching academic essay writing is the **structured paragraph method.** This involves teaching you about the elements that go into a standard academic paragraph or what is normally described as an essay's **body paragraph.** After the student has written countless body paragraphs and developed flair and lots of confidence, we can proceed to the other aspects of the essay like the **introduction** and **conclusion**.

According to *Webster's New College Dictionary*, a paragraph is "**a distinct division of a written work or composition that expresses a thought or point relevant to the whole but is**

complete in itself and may consist of one or more sentences" (815). In simpler terms, this means a paragraph is made up of two or more sentences that express a **main** or **single idea** or concept. It can be any number of sentences but still hold a single idea. But for our purposes, three to six sentences will be enough.

But why has it assumed such importance in our lives?

Because, it is the most essential component in every essay, article, speech, journal or piece of writing. Every essay or composition is judged—among other criteria—on the strength of its paragraphs. In fact, the person who learns how to create the best or most effective paragraphs will probably write the best essays in class—or anywhere else!

Let me illustrate this point using two different paragraphs. Each of these paragraphs will attempt to express the single idea that one main advantage of a having a car is that it saves you an enormous amount of time in transportation.

Example 1:

A car is faster than most forms of transportation. It has an engine and uses fuel so one does not have to worry about losing stamina, which would be the case if you are riding a horse. For this reason, a car saves you a lot of time in transportation.

Example 2:

One of the main advantages of having a car is that it saves you a lot of time. That is to say, because it is powered by an engine, a car can get you to your destination more quickly than most forms of transportation. This results in a lot of time-saving. For example, if Eric has to travel twenty miles to deliver a parcel, he will certainly do it faster by a car than riding a bike or horse.

A quick glance at the two examples above will tell you that the more effective or better-written paragraph is Example 2.

What makes Example 2 a better paragraph than Example 1? What are the elements or components of a good paragraph? What is the structure of the paragraph? How do you put it together in such an effective manner that anyone reading it—whether he is a college professor or a guy in the street—is left in no doubt that it is a good paragraph that clearly expresses that single idea?

Most writers will tell you about the first element in the structured paragraph, which is the topic sentence. The other elements are expressed in vague concepts like "details," "body" or "chronological importance." They fail to give the student specifics. And this is where the **Arloo Essay Matrix®** has proved so useful.

THE ARLOO ESSAY MATRIX®

The Arloo Essay Matrix is a unique approach to essay writing for college students. It is an essay writing method that cuts through the layers of course material and textbook information to get to the purest elements of the paragraph. And it is so effective that anybody with average writing skills can master the techniques.

In this chapter, I will show you how the matrix works in the **body paragraph**. In subsequent chapters, I will demonstrate how it works in the **conclusion**, before rounding it off with its application in the **introduction**, particularly in coming up with the **thesis statement**.

The Elements of the Paragraph:

According to the Arloo Essay Matrix, there are three elements in a properly structured paragraph:
1. The topic sentence
2. The explanation
3. The evidence or support

Every effective paragraph has these three elements. This means, if you master the Arloo Matrix, you can tackle any academic writing assignment with ease. And it is called a "**matrix**" because it serves as a mold or design which can hold or generate various types of paragraphs, whether you are writing an argumentative, narrative, descriptive, process or any other type of essay.

The **topic sentence** typically states the main idea in the paragraph. This is usually the main point which was written down in the outline. The **explanation** breaks down this main idea and explains it. It builds up the argument set out in the topic sentence through deductive reasoning. The result is that it expands and develops the paragraph into a more logical, coherent unit. The last element—**the evidence or support**—provides solid proofs from one's readings, textbook or peer-reviewed journals to support the main idea set out in the topic sentence. Other sources of evidence or support are expert testimony, personal experience, analogies, facts and statistics, field research and shared values (Wysocki and Lynch 104).

In their book, *The Composition of Everyday Life*, John Mauk and John Metz make an interesting case for the standard body paragraph (256).

Although they concede that every writer may choose his own preference, they suggest that every paragraph should have this structure:
i. Main idea or Topic Sentence
ii. Evidence (support)
iii. Evidence (support)
iv. Explanation

There is nothing wrong with this strategy since it contains all the elements of a structured paragraph—topic sentence, evidence, and explanation. I prefer, however, to go with the Arloo Essay Matrix, which employs the following strategy:
i. Main idea or topic sentence
ii. Explanation
iii. Evidence (support)

My reasons are simple. First of all, this approach helps you to avoid the *fallacy of cause and effect*. Let me digress a bit.

One of the goals of academic work is to help you sharpen your mind as a **critical thinker**. Critical thinking is defined as analyzing, evaluating, and synthesizing information into logical conclusions. Hence, part of your academic training is how to recognize **logical fallacies**, which simply refer to a **flaw or error in the structure of an argument or deductive reasoning that makes a claim invalid**. There are a whole lot of them in Mauk and Metz's book, including fallacies of hasty generalization, the straw person, oversimplification, false analogy, and the like (252). But the one that concerns us most, as far as paragraph development is concerned, is the fallacy of cause and effect.

This fallacy assumes a causal relationship between two events because they occur together. That is, because event A took place before event B, then it stands to reason that A caused B. For example, if there is a car crash after a drop in temperature, then the drop in temperature might have caused the crash. But this is an invalid deduction.

In our discussion of the body paragraph, we mentioned that the explanation explains and expands the topic sentence. In other words, the explanation expands the topic sentence through deductive reasoning, creating a "cause-and-effect" between the two elements. Thus, when our explanation follows logically from the topic sentence (i.e. the claim), then it holds true and becomes a valid argument. But when the explanation is not logically deduced from the topic sentence, it leads to the fallacy of cause and effect.

In terms of critical thinking, therefore, this paragraph structure—topic sentence, explanation, and evidence—is more useful for writing essays: it helps you avoid the fallacy of cause and effect.

Let us look at this example:

> *Lastly, domestic violence leads to huge financial losses for the nation.* **The point is that when domestic violence incidents occur, it involves not only the partners directly concerned but also the law enforcement officers called in, the lawyers handling the disputes and a lot of other things. It also means hospital bills and time lost from work by both abusers and victims. All these add to a huge financial cost to the country, valuable resources which could have been used to provide jobs and services for people.** *Citing a study by Walby (2004), Gibbons reports that the UK government spends about three billion pounds a year on domestic violence services alone (12).*

In the above example, the explanation—the bold typeface—follows logically, or is deduced from the main idea or topic sentence of the paragraph (which has been underlined).

On the other hand, if the explanation had not followed deductively from the claim made in the topic sentence, then the whole paragraph would have been an invalid argument. This is why an ability to identify the fallacy of cause and effect is so crucial in essay writing and, by extension, critical thinking.

And that is the reason why I recommend the Arloo Matrix's body paragraph structure (i.e. topic sentence, explanation, and evidence) to students of essay writing. By mastering it, you develop the habit of making deductive judgments in your academic readings and writings, thereby making you a better scholar. And, in a world where critical thinking is a valued commodity, this ability is priceless.

In addition to training you in deductive reasoning, the Arloo Matrix helps you take notes effectively in your studies. The reason is that it helps you recognize the topic sentence (i.e. the main idea or point) in every paragraph of your study material. These main points then become the core of your note-taking.

Another reason I prefer this approach to Mauk and Metz's version is that you become very skillful at presentations—and at making impromptu speeches—since deductive abilities become a habit.

*

At its most primary level, this is how the body paragraph in the Arloo Matrix works. Suppose I want to write an essay about the causes of crime. Let us say I come up with two causes of crime:

1. Unemployment
2. Greed

In writing out my essay, each of these causes will become the topic sentence of a paragraph. (Note that these examples are more like opinion essays and are for illustration only. The typical college essay is a little more complex). Now, let us apply the Arloo Matrix:

Example 1.

One of the most common causes of crime is unemployment. In other words, a person without a job or any means of income still has to pay his bills. Since he has no money, he thinks the easiest way to get it is by stealing or robbery. This may cause him to steal. For instance, in 2011, an unemployed man robbed a bank in New York for money to buy medicine.

In the above paragraph, the first sentence— "One of the most common causes of crime is unemployment"—serves as the topic sentence. The next three sentences constitute the explanation. The last sentence is the evidence.

Let us look at the second cause of crime—greed—and apply the Arloo Matrix.

Example 2:

Another cause of crime is greed. A person may like to have more things than he or she can afford. Since the person does not have enough money, he or she may try to shoplift these from a supermarket or a store, leading to a criminal act. For instance, a number of people caught shoplifting do so from pure greed, since some of the stolen items are things they already have

Here too, the first sentence is the topic sentence. The next two make up the explanation while the last sentence represents the evidence.

In subsequent chapters, we will examine the Arloo Matrix in more detail by looking at each element separately.

In order to illustrate and clarify my principles, I have added two complete college level essays in the Appendices to this book. Refer to them as much as you can because all the principles I am teaching in the first part of this book—The Standard Academic Essay—have been applied in writing these essays.

The first one in Appendix I—the **opinion essay**—is like those you normally write as part of your college application process. It is also similar to the questions you tackle at the SAT, ACT, GED, and other examinations for high school students. Quite a few of the essays you will write in your college freshman year will be of this type.

The second one, which I will describe as the **standard academic college essay** or **research paper**, is not much different from the opinion essay. But it demands actual proofs, citations, facts and statistics, and research from your college textbooks and journals. Hence, while you can use examples from everyday experiences, analogies, shared values, popular culture, and stories as evidence in the opinion essay, the only evidence or support permitted in the standard academic essay must come from your approved textbooks and peer-reviewed journals (i.e. scholarly journals).

EXERCISES

The major elements of the Arloo Essay Matrix—topic sentence, the explanation, and the evidence—actually work and can be applied to every type of writing, even top-notch professional articles in publications like TIME magazine. I want you to go online and do something for me. Look up the following sections in past publications of TIME

Magazine (www.time.com). Examine each paragraph closely. Try and identify:

i. The topic sentence
ii. The explanation
iii. The evidence

1. Name of Article: "The Senate's China Misstep"
Author: Rana Foroohar
Date of Issue: October 24, 2011. Vol 178, No. 16
Page 17, paragraphs 3, 4, and 6.

In paragraph 3 of Foroohar's article on the trade battle between the United States and China, you will find that the first sentence is the topic sentence. The next two make up the explanation while the last sentence represents the evidence (Rana Foroohar 17).

In paragraph 4, the first sentence is the topic sentence, the next one is the explanation and the last sentence is the evidence (Foroohar 17). Paragraph 6 also has a very good example of a topic sentence. It is followed by a very solid explanation in the next two sentences. The last two sentences which contain quotes make up the evidence.

2. Name of Article: "The Most Important Man in Europe"

Author: Michael Schuman
Date of Issue: February 20, 2012 (Vol 179, No. 7)
Page 28, paragraph 3.

In Michael Schuman's article on Mario Monti, Italy's new Prime Minister, the first sentence of paragraph 3 is a good example of a topic sentence. The next sentence is the explanation and the final sentence is the evidence.

You can look up other articles in respected magazines and try to identify the three elements.

CHAPTER 2

THE TOPIC SENTENCE–ROLE OF TRANSITIONS

As I mentioned earlier, our approach to essay writing begins with writing lots of body paragraphs. Once you master these, we can move to the introduction and conclusion.

The body paragraph almost always begins with a topic sentence which contains the *key* or *main idea* in the paragraph. This main idea is the one that was written down when you developed and wrote out your essay's outline. Therefore, in order to demonstrate how the topic sentence works, we will select a sample essay topic and create a formal outline.

But even before writing the formal essay outline, we need to have a strategy for breaking down an essay topic into its relevant parts or **core demands**. In other words, what's the essay about? Is it asking you to discuss the **reasons** why a particular law was passed? Or, is it asking for the **factors** or **reasons** that led to a demonstration against a government program?

Most essay questions deal with an aspect of a topic, issue, theory or concept. The first thing to do, therefore, is to break the question down to its basic components. In effect, you **will** determine whether the question is asking for causes, effects, reasons, principles, features, similarities, differences, advantages and disadvantages, or any aspect that relates to the topic under discussion.

Let me illustrate this point with a few essay questions and show you how to break them down:

1. *Write an essay about the factors leading to the collapse of the Ottoman Empire.*
This essay is asking for the causes or reasons why the Ottoman Empire collapsed.

2. *Explain why immigration reform is such a difficult policy to implement.*
This question is asking for reasons why immigration reform has not been successful.

3. *"It is very desirable to have trade agreements with other countries." Discuss.*
This one is asking for the benefits or advantages of trade agreements.

4. *Examine the impact of the 2008 Recession on Americans.*

This essay topic is asking for the <u>effects</u> of the recent recession on Americans.

    Once your essay topic has been broken down into its basic components, the next thing to do is to write out the essay outline. There are basically two kinds of essay outlines—the informal and the formal outline. The informal outline, which does not have a rigid structure, helps you to come up with ideas in planning your essay. The formal outline, on the other hand, is very structured and has specific formatting rules.

    For more on informal outlines, I would advise you to consult your English professor or some course-approved textbooks for ideas. There are a lot of resources online too. My main focus is on how to write a formal outline since it helps to structure and organize your essay.

    The first thing to note about the formal outline is that every major section of your paper should be labeled with a Roman numeral (i.e. I, II, III, IV, etc). By major section, we are referring to the introduction, body, or conclusion of your essay.

    Second, each subsection of a major section should be labeled with a capital letter (A, B, C, etc).

The subsection of the introduction comprises the components or elements that make up an essay's introduction. These include the thesis statement and the topic's definition where applicable. Similarly, in the body of the essay, subsections may include the causes, factors, positive or negative effects of an event, and so on, as we discussed on the previous two pages. In the conclusion, the subsections may include an affirmation of the thesis statement and a summary of the main points used in the essay.

Lastly, each sub-subsection should be labeled with an Arabic numeral (i.e. 1, 2, 3, etc). These sub-subsections, from experience, are mainly found in the body of the essay. Here, an essay may ask you to discuss, for example, three advantages or benefits of the topic under discussion. This sub-subsection allows you to break down the essay's body into the three advantages or benefits the question is asking for.

One important fact you should know about the formal outline is that for each major section, subsection or sub-subsection, you cannot have an I without an II. You cannot also have an A without a B, or a 1 without a 2. This simply means that no major section (I, II, etc), subsection (A, B, etc) or sub-subsection (1, 2, etc) can be made up of only a single point. If it is made up of a single point, then it is unnecessary to subdivide it. Hence, the rule: every I must have II, every A, a B, and so on.

This is how a formal outline looks like:

FORMAL OUTLINE

I. Major Section (Introduction)
    A. Thesis Statement
    B. Definition of Topic

II. Major Section (Body)
    A. Supporting Arguments
       1. First supporting argument
       2. Second supporting argument
       3. Third supporting argument
    B. Opposing Arguments (Optional)
       1. First opposing argument
       2. Second opposing argument
       3. Third opposing argument

III. Major Section (Conclusion)
    A. Summary of arguments
    B. Re-statement and affirmation of Thesis

Now, we will select a typical college-freshman essay topic paraphrased from a college instructor's class assignment (Caroline Quaas 2):

SAMPLE OPINION ESSAY TOPIC

Write a paper explaining and defining one of your character traits. Include what you think it means to have a particular trait and how it affects or influences certain areas of your life. Explore your trait's effects on family, school, work, relationships, community, etc.

Looking at our sample opinion essay topic (Refer to Appendix I for the complete essay), we can see that the question's **core demand** is about character traits and how they influence interactions with our family, work, friendship and community. Thus, in our essay, we will have to define "character traits" and set out their effects in our lives and relationships.

FORMAL OUTLINE
I. Introduction
   A. Thesis Statement: My persistence, more than any other character trait, has helped me overcome obstacles to become a successful student.
   B. Definition of Character Traits
II. Body
   A. Positive Effects
      1. Family—Role model to younger siblings
      2. School—Hardworking and consistent
      3. Work—Diligent in my tasks

      4. Community—Youth volunteer

   B. Negative Effects

      1. Social life—Lonely and shunned by peers

      2. Church life—Under suspicion by peers

III. Conclusion

   A. Summary of positive and negative effects

   B. Re-statement and affirmation of Thesis

This essay topic is the first of two examples that will be used to illustrate how the matrix works in the development of the body paragraph, which—as already mentioned—is made up of three elements:

1. The topic sentence

2. The explanation

3. The evidence (support)

In order to get the full benefits of the Arloo Essay Matrix, I will suggest that you pick an essay topic of your own—either from your English essay textbook or online—and apply the ideas you will learn from our illustrations as we tackle the body paragraphs, the conclusion, and the introduction. This way, by the time we come to the end of the first part of the book, you will have written a complete standard essay by yourself. This will give you a valuable hands-on experience with the main ideas in the book. And the boost to your self-confidence will be immense.

*

Of the three elements that make up the structured paragraph, the easiest—and most important—to understand is the topic sentence. It is always the *sentence* or *idea* that was written down in the essay outline. It also contains the main idea or concept in the paragraph and is the reason why the other elements exist. To put it another way, the other elements function solely to expand on the topic sentence. On some occasions, the topic sentence appears at the end of the paragraph but that takes a certain level of mastery. For now, we will stick to the usual approach, which is to bring it at the beginning of the paragraph.

The other thing to know about the topic sentence is that when it appears at the beginning of the paragraph in a multi-paragraph essay, it often begins with a **transition**. *Transitions are words or phrases that help you to link up sentences or paragraphs smoothly without breaking the chain of thought or idea*. They can also signal a change in the direction of an argument in an essay. A list of transitions can be found in various chapters of this book as you read along. Here are some examples:

FREQUENTLY USED TRANSITIONS
First of all…
In the first place…
Firstly…
Secondly…
Next…
Thirdly…
Moreover…
Furthermore…
In addition…
Not only…but…
Finally…
Lastly…

Let us have some practice with the topic sentence and transitions as we develop our sample essay's body paragraphs. Note that even though we are skipping the introduction of this essay, we will still need a working definition of "trait" to write meaningful paragraphs. Based on this, we will define a trait generally as "an attribute of character or personality that reveals a person's beliefs and values and tells us what type of person he or she is, whether that person is lazy or hardworking, mean or kind, honest or a cheat." A person's traits show how that person will typically behave when faced with certain situations. So when we describe someone as being a coward—which is a character trait—we are predicting that whenever such a person is faced with a situation that calls for courage, he or she will act in a cowardly way. For instance, if that person is asked to go into a dark house by himself, he or she will make up an excuse not to because of fear.

Note that this is a working definition for essay-writing purposes only. For a more detailed definition of trait, look it up in a dictionary or textbook.

In our outline, we wrote down four ways a particular character trait has affected and influenced certain areas of our lives: family, relationships, school and community. Let us see how transitions can help us develop good topic sentences.

EXAMPLE 1:

My persistence has had a great impact on my life. ***One of the ways* it has influenced my life is that it has helped me to be a role model to my younger siblings.** Being the eldest child, my parents have always taught me to serve as a great example to my siblings. Although I could not read very well in elementary school, I enrolled at the library and brought some books home. It was difficult at first but with a dictionary and some help from my parents I was able to read all the books.

This encouraged me to read more. By the time I reached middle school, I was reading the scriptures in church. My siblings were so impressed that they all got books from the library and started reading.

The bold type in the above paragraph is the topic sentence. The italicized phrase at the beginning of the topic sentence is the transition. The sentence preceding the topic sentence is a general statement you make before tackling a major section of your essay (Note: you usually make this sweeping general statement right before discussing the individual points in a major section of your essay). As you can see here, the topic sentence contains the <u>main idea</u> in the paragraph. The six sentences that follow expand and flesh out this idea.

Still using our sample essay topic, let us try another example:

Example 2:

Secondly, my persistence has influenced my life in school. I'm not the brightest student in class. But whenever I'm given a class assignment, I start work on it the same day. I make sure I get the necessary books and follow the instructions carefully. And I always turn my work in on time. Because of this my teachers always praise me and tell others to follow my example. In my last year in Junior high school, for instance, I got an award for always turning my work in before everybody else.

Here too, the bold typeface is the topic sentence while the italicized section is the transition. Again, the rest of the paragraph fleshes out the main idea captured in the topic sentence. Let us try two more illustrations:

Example 3:

My persistence has had an effect *not only* on my relationships *but also* on my job. But in this case, it has been positive. I work in an electronics assembly plant. The work is difficult and complicated. But I make sure I learn every operation till I am perfect at it. And I always do a quality check. Some of my colleagues don't take the trouble to check for quality and are always warned about their attitude. As a result of this, last week there were a lot of lay-offs but I kept my job due to my persistent attitude for quality work.

Example 4 (This time, try to identify the topic sentence and the transition by yourself):

Lastly, my persistence has led to my elevation as the head of the Volunteers Club at my church. In every my church, there are always lots of activities and events going on. I volunteered a lot of my time for these activities. If I did not have the resources or knowledge for an assignment, I made sure that I used every means at my disposal to get the problem solved. After a very difficult Christmas play which I helped to stage, our pastor called me into his office and asked me to set up a Volunteers' Club. At first people didn't want to join. But I knocked on their doors and called their telephones so many times that they gave in. Now, we do a lot of things to help our community. For example, every last Saturday of the month, we have a Clean-up, clearing weeds and sweeping up trash to beautify the neighborhood.

Mastering these transitions will help you in a lot of ways as you strive for the winning essay. They will help you in:
1. Writing solid topic sentences that effortlessly link your ideas and paragraphs.
2. Writing effective and catchy introductions.
3. Developing the thesis statement.
4. Writing great conclusions.

Transitions help to link paragraphs together. But one of their most effective uses is to help the student switch from one side of an argument to the other. We will discuss this in more detail when we come to the section on conclusions and introductions.

One thing you should note, however, is that not every paragraph begins with a transition. One reason for this is to avoid boredom and predictability. To achieve this, you go ahead and write your paragraph with the transition during your first draft. Then, remove it when you do the second draft. Of course, be mindful of your grammar and syntax.

Let us look at four examples that illustrate the topic sentence and transitions. The first two contain transitions. I took the first two from actual essays I submitted as class assignments in my Master's degree program. The third one is quoted from an entertainment blog. The topic sentences are in bold type and transitions are italicized:

1.   **The role of environmental stress has been cited as *another cause* of Generalized Anxiety Disorder or GAD (Endler & Edwards, 1988; Monroe & Wade, 1988).** That is to say, many patients experience significant negative and

unexpected events in the months before their conditions become pathological (Blazer, Hughes & George, 1987). These stressors include job difficulties, personal loss, interpersonal problems, physical illness or adjustment to new environments ("The Perils of Generalized Anxiety Disorder" 5).

2. *One main* **criticism against Rogers is that he could not explain Actualization in precise terms.** This makes it difficult to generate research from the theories. For instance, to study self-actualization, you need to know which aspect of a subject's life was actualizing so that you can focus. The second criticism was that if everyone was self-actualizing uninhibitedly, living life to the fullest—regardless of the effects on other people—it would lead to conflict and chaos (Is Personality Fixed in Childhood? 6).

3. **"Aboodatoi" appears to be the missing link in previous attempts to trace the roots of Hip-hop in Africa, most notably in Kwaw Ansah's epic film, "Crossroads of People, Crossroads of Trade" (1994).** In Kwaw Ansah's documentary, he makes the case that clap-and-dance games played by native African girls form the roots of hip-hop music. But I think a stronger case

can be made for Jama music with respect to the similarities between Jama and hip-hop in terms of themes, structure, content, choric style and group-performance. And, more than any hiplife song to date, "Aboodatoi" exemplifies this unique fusion between traditional African rhythms and Hip-hop (Gasmilla 1).

EXERCISES

Go online and look for about three standard (i.e. non-narrative or non-descriptive) college essay topics and do the following:

1. Break down each topic to determine whether it's about reasons, factors, causes, advantages, features, impressions, etc.

2. Develop a formal outline for each essay topic.

3. Create a topic sentence for each point in the outline.

CHAPTER 3

THE EXPLANATION–SEQUENTIAL TRANSITIONS

I am sure you have seen an MTV interview where the phrase "Y'know what I'm saying?" kept popping up anytime the musician tried to explain a point he had made. And I am also sure there have been occasions when you have told someone a fact and the person had asked you to explain what you meant. Well, that is what the second element of the Arloo Matrix—the explanation—is all about; it allows you to explain the topic sentence, or the main idea you are trying to get across, in greater detail.

This segment of the paragraph is where you develop your main or key point and build up your argument into a coherent unit. In fact, this is the "development" part of your body paragraph, where you use the logic of deductive reasoning to prove the main idea. In deductive reasoning, you draw a specific conclusion based on a general premise, claim or idea. Thus, whenever you explain or break down the main idea in your topic sentence, you are using deductive reasoning to draw a conclusion that is based on the main idea or claim in the topic sentence (Kenneth Mai 1). To put it more simply, your explanation is a deduction that is premised on the topic sentence. This element is crucial for any structured paragraph.

There is nothing difficult about this segment, but I have found that it throws a lot of you off, causing you to give long-winded explanations that ultimately fail to make sense.

In order to solve this problem, I have compiled a list of what is called deductive phrases or what Kenneth Mai describes as **sequential transitions** (1). They function as *transitional phrases* that initiate the explanation and help with the deductive process. Sometimes, a student feels apprehensive that people may laugh at his or her attempts to explain a topic sentence. But a thorough knowledge of sequential transitions helps you develop the competence needed to write your own explanations. In other words, they function like "baby walkers" for you till your feet are strong enough. Then you can discard them and walk, strut and even dance to the rhythms of your writing. Still, I have found them very useful in a lot of assignments, like two sentences above.

Some examples of sequential transitions are shown below:

SEQUENTIAL TRANSITIONS

In other words...

That is to say...

The point being made is...

The point is that...

What I'm trying to say is that...

What I mean is that...

This implies that...

The implication here is that...

This involves...

In effect...

In short...

The fact is...

This indicates that...

It follows that...

Let us get back to the essay on Character Traits (Refer to Appendix I). In the third paragraph—the first body paragraph—my topic sentence mentions that my persistence has helped me become a role model to my siblings. In explaining how this came about, I will have to show a direct, causal link between my success in learning how to read and how it impressed my siblings. This is where the sequential transition becomes useful: it helps to draw a direct, logical line between the topic sentence and the explanation on how I became a role model.

Example 1:

My persistence has had a great impact on my life. One of the ways it has influenced my life is that it has helped me to be a role model to my younger siblings. ***That is to say,*** **being the eldest child, my parents have always taught me to serve as a great example to my siblings. Although I could not read very well in elementary school, I enrolled at the library and brought some books home. It was difficult at first but with a dictionary and some help from my parents I was able to read all the books. This encouraged me to read more. By the time I reached middle school, I was reading the scriptures in church. My siblings were so impressed that they all got books from the library and started reading.** My seven-year-old sister, for example, reads a new book every week.

In the above paragraph, the bold typeface represents the explanation of the topic sentence. The italicized words are the sequential transitions. Let us look at two more examples below:

Example 2:

Secondly, my persistence has influenced my progress in school. ***The point I am trying to make is that* I am not the brightest student in class. But whenever I am given a class assignment, I start work on it the same day. I make sure I get the necessary books and follow the instructions carefully. And I always turn my work in on time. Because of this my teachers always praise me and tell others to follow my example.** In my last year in Junior high school, for instance, I got an award for always turning my work in before everybody else did.

Example 3:

My persistence has had an impact not only in school but a positive effect on my job as well. ***The point is that,* I work in an electronics assembly plant where the work is difficult and complicated. But I make sure I learn every operation till I am perfect at it. And I always do a quality check. Some of my colleagues don't take the trouble to check for quality and are always warned about their attitude. As a result of this, last week there were a lot of lay-offs but I kept my job due to my persistent attitude for quality work.** Another instance was when my Line

Supervisor praised me on my perfect attendance record during a weekly meeting.

Now, try and identify the sequential transition and the explanation in the next paragraph. Use different colors to highlight them:

Lastly, my persistence has led to my elevation as the head of the Volunteers Club at my church. The fact is every church has lots of activities and events going on at any point in time. I volunteer a lot of my time for these activities. One day, after a very difficult Christmas play which I helped to stage, our pastor called me into his office and asked me to set up a Volunteers' Club. At first people didn't want to join. But I knocked on their doors and called their phones so many times that they gave in. Now, we do a lot of things to help our community. For example, every last Saturday of the month, we have a Clean-Up exercise, clearing weeds and sweeping up trash to beautify the neighborhood.

Let us look at some examples of sequential transitions in some of my own essays. Again, they are in italics. The bold typeface makes up the explanation of the topic sentence:

1.   Knowledge of the individual and environmental factors that impact on subjective well-being and wellness will go a long way to reframe and refocus the orientations counselors adopt to manage their clients. *In other words*, **there is a need to do away with the pathological and embrace the salutogenic.** Four main approaches that come to mind in this direction are education, dissemination of literature, behavioral interventions and cognitive therapies (<u>Positive Psychology and Wellness</u> 4).

2.   Beck (1993) mentions the application of cognitive approaches to facilitate wellness. *This implies that* **changing the mindset through cognitive reframing and restructuring will help clients think, feel and behave more positively**. Rational Emotive Therapy as proposed by Ellis (1997) would be a useful tool in this direction. Thus major ideas like optimism, self-determination, self-efficacy, flow and adaptive mechanisms could be taught to clients through a conscious individual or group therapy approach for optimum results. Although the issue of negative societal attitudes persists, if clients inculcate these concepts effectively through therapy, they would, to a large extent, be immune from these attitudes, since their

motivation would be intrinsic (<u>Positive Psychology</u> 5).

Now let us go back to our essay on Character Traits (Refer to Appendix I). The second part of the essay deals with the negative effects of my persistence. Study the paragraphs carefully and notice how they have been developed. You can practice highlighting the sequential transitions and the explanations.

I am sure someone is screaming now: "If everyone reading this book uses the same sequential transitions, won't all essays look the same?"

The answer is "No."

One reason is that writers and students have been using the same words, phrases and idioms of the English language for hundreds of years. Yet each writer has a distinct voice. Even when lesser writers try to imitate others, they sound different. So there is no fear of that happening.

Secondly, in your bid to deduce a causal relationship from the topic sentence, it is desirable to telegraph your punches at times. That is to say, when you are dealing with a dense, complicated subject, it is good to signal that you are trying to explain an idea or concept to the reader. From that angle, therefore, it is not always a bad thing to use the sequential transition. They help to ease the burden of proof, so to speak.

On a more practical level, however, this problem can be fixed in a very simple way. Remember I mentioned "baby walkers" earlier in the chapter. Well, sequential transitions function like walkers for the freshman writer—they prop up your explanations. As soon as you become adept at explaining and building up your topic sentences or key points in a paragraph, you can stop using them. Ideally, I would recommend that you use them in the first draft of the essay. When you are satisfied that the paragraph is tight and stands on its own, you can drop the phrases, as shown in the following examples. In both examples, the sequential transition in the first draft is in bold italics. In the second draft, it has been taken out:

Example 1:
First Draft:

Secondly, my persistence has influenced my life in school. ***The point I am trying to make is that*** I'm not the brightest student in class. But whenever I'm given a class assignment, I start work on it the same day. I make sure I get the necessary books and follow the instructions carefully. And I always turn my work in on time. Because of this my teachers always praise me and tell others to follow my example. In my last year in Junior high school, for instance, I got an award for always turning my work in before everybody else.

Second Draft:

Secondly, my persistence has influenced my life in school. I'm not the brightest student in class. But whenever I'm given a class assignment, I start work on it the same day. I make sure I get the necessary books and follow the instructions carefully. And I always turn my work in on time. Because of this my teachers always praise me and tell others to follow my example. In my last year in Junior high school, for instance, I got an award for always turning my work in before everybody else.

Example 2:
First Draft:

Secondly, we can deal with domestic violence by enacting stricter laws and penalties for those who commit these acts. ***This implies that*** the stricter the laws against domestic violence, the more deterrent they will be to would-be offenders. These will scare spouses from attacking each other. Thus, the rate of attacks will be reduced, if not eliminated.

Second Draft:

Secondly, we can deal with domestic violence by enacting stricter laws and penalties for those who commit these acts. The stricter the laws against domestic violence, the more deterrent they will be to would-be offenders. These will scare spouses from attacking each other. Thus, the rate of attacks will be reduced, if not eliminated.

The Arloo Matrix® is by no means a rigid system in which every explanation is made up of four, five or seven sentences. It all depends on the academic level of the student and the type of essay; where a college freshman is fine with two or three sentences for the explanation segment, an advanced student may need four or more. And these sequential transitions go a long way in bringing out the logic in your explanations.

EXERCISES

Go back to the outlines you developed at the end of Chapter 2 and:

1. Using a sequential transition to begin each explanation, develop and explain each topic sentence you wrote for the 3 essay topics. The

explanations should be between three to five sentences long.

2. Do a second draft of your essay. This time, drop all the sequential transitions. Does it work?

CHAPTER 4

THE EVIDENCE–OPINION VS ACADEMIC ESSAY

The last component of the Arloo Matrix in the body paragraph is the **evidence** or **support** for the topic sentence. In many ways, this is the most exciting part of the matrix. For the opinion essay, this is where you reach into your memory bank of all the stories, movies, news items, books and neighborhood gossip for an example, an instance, or a case that validates or supports the reason, factor, cause or problem you have mentioned in your topic sentence.

It is an easy task if you have mastered your matrix. If not, do not sweat it. You can do one of the following:

1. Try to remember all the movies you have seen. You will surely come up with a character or scene to support your topic sentence or main point. This is acceptable in a college freshman opinion essay, SAT, TOEFL or GED essay.

2. Try and recall all the news items you have seen or heard of on CNN, MSNBC, ABC, BBC, Fox and

the like. They will give you a vivid example or instance to use.

3. Rake up any and everything you ever read in a novel, textbook, newspaper or magazine, not forgetting the internet.

4. From now on, make it a special point of taking note of everything you read or hear in your world, whether at work, school, church, TV, online, in music or wherever people exchange information. It may be a life-saver in an exam.

Giving evidence or support in a standard academic essay, however, is a different ball game. The only analogy I can make in the distinction between the evidence or support required in an opinion essay, and those required in an academic essay is to compare them to St. Paul's proverbial "milk and meat" Christians. With the former, any example goes, as long as it is relevant to the main idea or topic sentence in the paragraph. It is the reason why the opinion essay is mostly written by high school students and college freshmen. On that score, it could be compared to "milk."

But when it comes to giving the evidence or proof to support a main point in an academic essay, you have to give some "real meat and bones"! This is where your academic essay is "made" or "broken." It demands strong academic evidence, facts and statistics, and field research to support your explanations and drive home the main point of the paragraph. Failure to do so will reduce your essay to mere fluff or cotton candy; all form and no substance. Good academic sources give you reliable, accurate information based on solid research. In getting your examples, you can do the following:

1. Your sources for examples or proofs should come from peer-reviewed or scholarly journals. If unsure, ask for assistance at the library. Scan the titles and read the abstracts for relevant materials.

2. Scour through your college textbooks. Your semester course outline will furnish you with a list of approved books and journals.

3. The publications should be recent, preferably within the last five years.

Again, I have lined up some phrases that introduce your evidence and support. I call them the **evidence phrases**. Here are a few:

For example…

An example is…

For instance…

An instance is…

A case in point…

To use as an illustration, consider…
As an illustration…
By way of example, consider…
In a study…
One research found that…
Studies have shown that…
Research evidence shows that…
According to a report (one report)…

Once again, let us look at a couple of illustrations from our opinion and academic essays. The bold typeface will be the paragraph's evidence, which is introduced by the evidence phrase in italics. In order to have some variety, the evidence phrase is sometimes placed in the middle of the sentence:

OPINION ESSAY:

Example 1:

My persistence has had a great impact on my life. One of the ways it has influenced my life is that it has helped me to be a role model to my younger siblings. That is to say, being the eldest child, my parents have always taught me to serve as a great example to my siblings. Although I could not read very well in elementary school, I enrolled at the library and brought some books home. It was difficult at first but with a dictionary and some help from my parents I was able to read all the books. This encouraged me to read more. By the time I reached middle school, I was reading the scriptures in church. My siblings were so impressed that they all got books from the library and started reading. *For example*, **my seven-year-old sister reads a new book every week.**

Example 2:

2.   Secondly, my persistence has influenced my life in school. The point I am trying to make is that I am not the brightest student in class. But whenever I am given a class assignment, I start work on it the same day. I make sure I get the necessary books and follow the instructions carefully. And I always turn my work in on time. Because of this my teachers always praise me and tell others to follow my example. **In my last year in junior high school, *for instance*, I got an award for always turning my work in before everybody else.**

Example 3:

My persistence has had an impact not only in school but a positive effect on my job as well. In other words, I work in an electronics assembly plant where the work is difficult and complicated. But I make sure I learn every operation till I am perfect at it. And I always do a quality check. Some of my colleagues do not take the trouble to check for quality and are always warned about their attitude. As a result of this, last week there were a lot of lay-offs but I kept my job due to my persistent attitude for quality work. *Another instance is* **when my line supervisor praised me on my perfect attendance record during a weekly meeting.**

ACADEMIC ESSAY:

In the academic essay, support from your textbooks or scholarly journals are usually preceded by what we call **signal phrases.** You can still begin this component with a phrase like "For instance..." or "For example..." but I will suggest that you drop these and go straight to the signal phrases. These let your reader know that you are giving evidence from your research and quoting or citing studies from authorities. This list is by no means complete but some examples of signal phrases are:

In a study...

Citing from a study...

According to a study by...

Based on a research conducted by...

Research conducted by...

Let us look at three instances of the use of signal phrases to introduce evidence (i.e. authoritative evidence) in the academic essay. The entire sections in bold typeface make up the evidence or examples from your research supporting your main point in the paragraph. The signal phrases are in italics:

Example 1:

Domestic violence has caused and continues to create a lot of social problems. But some of the most devastating of these effects are loss of lives and permanent disability sustained by its victims. This implies that the violence between intimate partners and among family members causes a lot of harm and suffering to both victims and perpetrators. Citing studies by Boursnell and Prosser (2010), Lynda Gibbons observes that a lot of domestic attacks involves "slapping, kicking, hitting, punching, burning or scalding, use of weapons or destruction of property; it often results in injury and can lead to death" (12). *According to Gibbons*, **in the UK the Home Office reported that of all the murder cases reported in 2011, 76% of women and 50% of men were killed by people known to the victims (12).**

Example 2:

Another effect of domestic violence is the devastating psychological effect it has on children. That is to say, most child victims of domestic violence suffer not only from physical, but also psychological and emotional trauma. *DeBoard-Lucas and Grych mention that* **about 7 million children in the United States live in houses of severe domestic violence (McDonald et al., 2006) in which one parent may beat or burn another, threaten with a weapon, or force them to do things against their will (343).** *He concludes that* **children practice what they see going on between parents when they grow up.** *This is supported by* **Moylan's findings that children exposed to domestic violence and or child abuse are more likely to show maladaptive behaviors during their teens and beyond (53).**

Example 3:

Lastly, domestic violence leads to huge financial losses for the nation. The point is that when domestic violence incidents occur, it involves not only the partners directly concerned but also the law enforcement officers called in, the lawyers handling the disputes and a lot of other things. It also means hospital bills and time lost from work by both abusers and victims. All these add to a huge financial cost to the country, valuable resources which could have been used to provide jobs and services for people. ***Citing a study by* Walby (2004), Gibbons reports that the UK government spends about three billion pounds a year on domestic violence services alone (12).**

As mentioned earlier, the Arloo Matrix is by no means a rigid system in which every paragraph is made up of a set number of sentences. It all depends on the academic level of the student and the type of essay.

Similarly, when it comes to the "evidence" segment, where the college opinion essay is fine with one or two sentences, the academic essay requires the student to cite one or two scholarly authorities in support of his topic sentences or main points. And there is nothing more exciting than when you discover the perfect research paper to support your main point.

One thing you should note is that every academic essay should have a **Works Cited** (MLA Style) or **Reference** (APA Style) page listing all the research sources (i.e. books, journals, publications and internet) you used in your research paper. You can have a look at the reference page at the end of the academic essay in Appendix I. Your professors will give you lots of assistance in this regard. They will also help you with your academic writing format. Find out from them whether you are using APA, MLA, CMS, or CSE style. You can purchase a Style Manual to help you with this task as well, or go online. These are very important aspects of college writing that the scope of this book does not cover.

*

These are just samples of the techniques I have developed to help you write that winning essay. These tools have been very effective in solving students' writing needs not only at the high school, GED, and college freshmen level but also at the Master's and Ph. D. levels. In fact, I would welcome the most hopeless cases (i.e. those who have not been able to write a decent essay, even with the help of the best instructors) so that I can demonstrate the effectiveness of my methods.

But everybody can benefit from my methods as well: bloggers, journalism students, broadcasters, speechwriters, politicians, ministers, lay preachers, and activists—the list is endless.

One of the most coveted talents in the world today is the capacity for critical thinking, which is roughly defined as the ability to think issues through, formulate solid opinions and theses, and express them succinctly or clearly in your writing, or at any forum or event. The methods I use help you to lay a solid foundation in critical thinking, regardless of what career you may choose, or what academic level you are operating on. And it is my fervent wish that you will succeed in your endeavor.

EXERCISES

Go back to the exercises at the end of Chapter 3.

1. For the three opinion essays you have been working on, develop the evidence to support each topic sentence and explanation you have written.

2. Select two academic essay topics and create formal outlines for them. Develop topic sentences and explanations for each point in your outline.

3. Go online or get a college textbook, do your research and develop the evidence to support your topic sentences and explanations.

CHAPTER 5

THE CONCLUSION –SIMPLIFYING IT

Summing up or concluding your essay is one of the most important components of essay writing. The reason is simple: it is the last paragraph in your essay so it leaves a lasting impression. According to Wysocki and Lynch, the conclusion helps in linking the main arguments of the essay to the topic by connecting the last sentence to the thesis of the essay (98). You should, therefore, use a lot of care in writing it. The main thing to remember is that this is where you summarize or review—in fresh words as much as you can—the main points or ideas used in your essay. After that, restate your thesis and affirm your arguments or position. Try and avoid lengthy conclusions since they may distract or dilute its impact.

Much noise has been made of the fact that using the phrase "In conclusion…" or "In summing up…" to begin your concluding paragraph is "artificial" (Kirszner & Mandell 45). I think it is a matter of opinion. For me, the freshman should master all the rules and apply them in lots of essays before attempting to break or walk away from them.

These phrases also signal that you have reached the end of your essay. On the other hand, if you feel the need to drop those phrases, a simple trick is to use them in the first draft of the conclusion. This puts you on solid ground while reviewing your main points and thesis statement. Once you are satisfied with your paragraph, you can drop them in your final draft, as I have done in the following example:

Step 1.

In summing up, I will say that my persistence has really made a difference in my life. Although it has sometimes made me lose friends and annoyed some people, it has also helped me to serve as a role model to my siblings, helped me to keep my job, and led to my leadership position in church. But what makes me very proud of this character trait is that, even though I was not the brightest boy in my high school class, I was able to score higher on my college entrance examinations than most of my classmates. And the only reason I was able to do this was because of my persistence.

Step 2:

I will say that my persistence has really made a difference in my life. Although it has sometimes made me lose friends and annoyed some people, it has also helped me to serve as a role model to my siblings, helped me to keep my job, and led to my leadership position in church. But what makes me very proud of this character trait is that, even though I was not the brightest boy in my high school class, I was able to score higher on my college entrance examinations than most of my classmates. And the only reason I was able to do this was because of my persistence.

Concluding your essay can be a lot of fun if you master the use of transitions. Transitions, as you already know, are words or expressions that show the relationships between paragraphs, ideas, causes and effects, comparisons and contrasts, reasons for or against, and the like (Kirszner & Mandell 41). But they are also very useful when it comes to weighing your final arguments. Kirszner & Mandell (42) give us a great list of some of these useful transitions listed below.

USEFUL TRANSITIONS FOR YOUR CONCLUSIONS

Beginning the paragraph	
To conclude	In sum
To sum up	Be that as it may
The final word…	

Making Comparison
Similarly
Likewise
In comparison

Contrast
On one hand…On the other hand…   But
Nevertheless   Yet
Still   Although
Instead   Nonetheless
Despite
However

Drawing a conclusion from two opposing
arguments (causes or effects)
Therefore
As a result
Be that as it may
Consequently
Subsequently

Let us have some more practice on writing
conclusions. Below are the outlines for a couple of
sample essays. In wrapping up or summing up these
two essays, we will review and evaluate the main
points to draw some conclusions. What we are
doing, in effect, is reaffirming our thesis with the

support of our main points or arguments. The use of transitions in this regard, is very useful and effective.

Example 1.
"ARMED ROBBERY IS GENETIC RATHER THAN A RESULT OF SOCIAL FACTORS." DO YOU AGREE?
OUTLINE
I. INTRODUCTION
Thesis Statement: Armed robbery is the result of social forces rather than genetic factors and needs a social approach to tackle it.
II. BODY
A. CAUSES
   1. Broken homes
   2. Lack of education
   3. Government policies

B. SOLUTIONS
   1. Stable marriages
   2. Good schools
   3. Public policy

III. CONCLUSION
       Having looked at these points outlined above, let us write a conclusion to the fictional

essay above. Remember, we are using transitions to help us do this. All transitions are in bold italics: Example 1.

In conclusion, it can be seen that the menace of armed robbery can be blamed on socio-economic forces rather than inherited genes. Its main causes are broken homes, lack of education and poor government policies. *Nevertheless*, the horrible effects of these causes can be reversed or minimized through social programs like stable marriages, good schools and sound public policies.

Example 2.

In summing up, it is clear that armed robbery, rather than being the result of genetic factors, can be blamed on socio-economic forces like broken homes, lack of education and poor government policies. The causes of armed robbery, *however,* can be removed or minimized through social approaches like stable marriages, good schools and sound government policies.

Let me use another example to drive home this point since it is one of the reasons most students score low marks in essay writing. This time, the outline shows the positive and negative sides of immigration.

Essay Question: *IS IMMIGRATION GOOD?*

<u>OUTLINE</u>

1. INTRODUCTION

<u>Thesis Statement</u>: Rather than being a negative phenomenon, immigration is a very positive thing and has been and continues to be a major force in nation-building.

II. BODY

A. POSITIVES

 1. More taxes

 2. Increase in consumer demand

 3. Increase in productivity

B. NEGATIVES

 1. Deflating the job market with cheap labor

 2. Increase in violence through gang activity

 3. Drain on health care

III. CONCLUSION

Sample *concluding* paragraph. The transitions are in bold italics.

    In conclusion, it can be seen that immigration has both good and bad sides. ***On one hand***, it leads to more tax revenue for the government, increases consumer demand, and raises productivity. ***On the other hand***, it is seen as a drain on health care, increases gang violence and is blamed for deflating the job market with low wages. *Be that as it may*, immigration has been and continues to be a major force in nation-building. It is up to the government to ensure that it reaps more of the positives than the negatives.

Let us look at examples from actual university-level essays and an entertainment blog.

1.   *There are a few recommendations* that counselors would do well to incorporate in their training and practice. *Among other suggestions*, they should understand the moral and religious convictions of the consumer and work within that context. They should never force clients to talk about sex nor hang their morality on the consumer. Neither should they threaten the consumer with seductive behavior or talk about their sexual experiences in an inappropriate manner. Sex is not an all-or-none experience; sexuality is more than a sex act. If a consumer cannot perform a certain sex act, he or she can do other things. The list of recommendations is endless but one thing counselors should always bear in mind is that talking about sex is all right; let people with disabilities know that they are sexual.

Intimacy is the goal (<u>Sexuality and Issues Related to Sexuality</u> 5).

2. ***But you can ignore*** all that has been said here about "Aboodatoi." ***You can ignore*** its homeopathic message and its link to the roots of Hip-hop in Africa. ***You can even choose to ignore*** its call to authenticity. ***But you can never forget*** its raw rhythms of happy feelings, its joie de vivre that—regardless of age—forces us into reminiscences of childhood, of a pristine period in our lives when we dared to be carefree and careless, wildly ululating on verdant communal playgrounds under bright moonlights before "progress" and technology ruined everything for us (<u>Gasmilla</u> 1).

From these examples, you can see that writing a well-developed, smart essay is not rocket science. I prefer to compare it to the logic of Math, specifically addition and subtraction: so many sentences make up a paragraph; so many paragraphs make up an essay, and so on. Once you know the rules and how to apply them, you are on your way to writing a winning essay.

<u>EXERCISES</u>

1. Practice your new skills on the use of transitions to write powerful paragraphs. Create your own fictional outlines like the ones on armed robbery and immigration and use the main points and thesis statements to write the conclusions.

2. Go back to the exercises at the end of Chapter 4. For each essay you are working on, write a conclusion.

3. For each conclusion, write a first draft using a transition. In the second draft, drop the transition.

4. I want us to repeat the exercise we did at the end of Chapter 1 involving the TIME Magazine articles. This time, we will look at two concluding paragraphs from two articles taken from TIME Magazine. The first is from a piece on the positive side of being an introvert (i.e. a quiet or shy person):

Name of Article: "Charms of the Quiet Child"
Author: Mehmet Oz
Date of Issue: February 6, 2012 (Vol 179, No. 5)
Page 46, Final paragraph.

In the last paragraph of this article, the writer sums up his arguments in the second sentence. This is then followed by a reaffirmation of the thesis statement in the next sentence: "All children have their own lens through which they view the world" (Mehmet Oz 46).

The second concluding paragraph is from an article on efforts to preserve Ecuador's portion of the Amazon Forest—the Yasuni National Park—from the destructive effects of oil drilling:

Name of Article: "Rain Forest for Ransom"
Author: Bryan Walsh
Date of Issue: February 6, 2012 (Vol 179, No. 5)
Page 39, Final paragraph

In this example, the main arguments are summed up in the first three sentences. The next two sentences reaffirm the thesis statement, which is underlined by the sentence: "Each of us benefits from the existence of forest reserves like Yasuni, and each of should share in the cost of preserving them" (Bryan Walsh 36).

CHAPTER 6

THE INTRODUCTION–THE THESIS STATEMENT

Writing a good introduction to your essay is one of the best things you can do as a student and I cannot emphasize it enough. For one thing, it gives the examiner a snapshot of your intelligence, verbal aptitude, and skill not only in essay writing, but in critical thinking as well. That is why, unlike most college textbooks, I did not bring this chapter at the beginning of the book: I wanted you to master transitions before teaching you the delicate art of writing introductions. This is very important because transitions play a major role in essay introductions, especially when it comes to writing the **thesis statement**. But before we tackle the thesis statement, let us see what makes an effective introduction.

Every essay introduction introduces the subject of the essay and states its **thesis** in a way that arouses the reader's interest and holds it for the rest of the essay. The thesis statement in particular prepares the reader and gives him certain expectations for your arguments or main ideas.

Failure to write a good introduction, therefore, means your essay is dead on arrival.

As stated before, my goal is to demystify the essay writing process for students so that every student (or people who just want to write for fun) can do so easily. A good chunk of this process is an effective introduction. An effective introduction also makes it easier for examiners and readers to understand the ideas or arguments the student is trying to convey. According to Wysocki and Lynch, a great introduction not only introduces the essay's subject matter by explicitly mentioning it; it also whets the reader's appetite by raising his curiosity about the main arguments (98).

I have noticed that most essay prompts are wordy and winding. This is especially true of SAT, GRE, college freshman, scholarship, and other competitive essays. This sometimes confuses the student. But, regardless of how confusing or wordy the essay prompts are, just remember that every essay deals with one or more aspects of a topical issue. These are known as the **core demands** or mandatory requirements of an essay. There are certain key words or phrases that help to identify these core demands. Learn to identify these key words in the essay questions or prompts, and half the job is done (We first touched on these key identifying words in Chapter 2).

COMMON KEY WORDS OR TOPICAL ISSUES IN ESSAY PROMPTS

Causes and/or effects of...(e.g. Voter suppression laws)

Reasons for/or against...(e.g. Why you respect our heroes)

Arguments in favor of/against...(e.g. Abortion)

Advantages and/or disadvantages...

Differences or similarities...

Types of...

Dangers of/associated with...

Characteristics of...

Aspects of...

Parts of...

Impressions of...

Features of...

Elements of...

Your main task as a student—whether in the examination room or ordinary class assignment—is to determine the core demands of the essay. In effect, you will analyze the question to find out if it is asking for causes, reasons, advantages, similarities, features, impressions or some other aspect of the topic.

Let us examine a few examples:

ESSAY #1.

"Does knowing people really well stop you from developing or maintaining respect for them?"

Support your position with reasoning and examples taken from your reading, studies, experience, or observations.

The above essay prompt is asking you about the **reasons** why familiarity breeds contempt or makes you lose respect for people. To write the essay, write an outline listing at least three or four reasons, as has been shown in previous chapters, and use the Arloo Matrix to develop your paragraphs. Do not forget that your outline comprises your introduction (which includes your thesis statement), body, and conclusion.

ESSAY #2:

"It is possible that, if people were encouraged to try things on their own and learn from their mistakes,

they'll achieve more in their life instead of simply relying on advice." Discuss.

This second prompt is talking about ways to achieve success on a stated goal. It is asking about the **advantages** of learning from the mistakes of your own efforts as against the **advantages** of relying on advice alone. Choose one side and sail with it. Your outline should include your introduction, body, and conclusion.

*

The next step after breaking down your essay topic is to set up your introduction in the Arloo Matrix:

THE ARLOO MATRIX:
1. The Topic Sentence
2. The Explanation
3. The Evidence

Remember, the topic sentence states the main idea in the paragraph. And, since this is the introduction, it is safe to say that the topic sentence—the main idea—is the **opening statement** of the essay. This opening statement also explicitly mentions the subject matter of the essay. For want of a better expression, I have named the opening statement **"The Attack."** The reason for this name is that it tackles or "confronts" the question or essay topic aggressively and, as it were, "beats it" into "submission."

How?

By tackling the question, you give yourself the upper-hand in steering and controlling the essay in any direction of your choice. Thus, instead of being a passive student, you become the master of your own fate! Let us look at a few examples:

Example 1.

Essay Topic: *"DRUG ABUSE CAN NEVER BE ERADICATED IN POOR NEIGHBORHOODS." Do you agree or disagree with this statement?*

Opening statement ("Attack"):

To state outright that drug abuse can never be eradicated in deprived neighborhoods is an extreme position unsupported by the facts at hand.

Example 2.

Essay Topic: *IS IMMIGRATION GOOD?*

Opening statement ("Attack"):

It is very easy to describe immigration as very bad for a country when one has not been well-informed on the various aspects of the issue.

As you can see, tackling the essay question or topic energizes you. It is almost as if you are throwing a challenge to the examiner or professor who gave you the question to write on. Do not be scared of this challenge—it is all good. And the best thing about it is that it energizes you to come up with some strong points to make good on your challenge. To facilitate this attack, I have compiled a list of phrases I call **"attack phrases."**

ATTACK PHRASES IN THE INTRODUCTION'S OPENING STATEMENT

1. It is one thing to say…
2. It is very easy to say…
3. It is tempting to see/judge…
4. It is tempting to describe…
5. To describe… (e.g. immigration) as… (e.g. a disaster) is…
6. To cast … (e.g. health care) in… (e.g. negative terms) is…

The second element of the Arloo Matrix—the explanatory part of the paragraph—is where you clarify and analyze the topic sentence. But there is an important difference between an essay's body paragraph and its introduction when it comes to applying the explanation component of the matrix.

Remember that in the body paragraph, we used **sequential transitions** to lead into the explanation. For example, we used phrases like "That is to say...," "This implies that...," "This involves...," "In other words..." and so on to signal the explanation.

In the case of the introductory paragraph, however, the explanatory segment begins with a different kind of phrase or transition which I have decided to name the **Introductory Transitional Phrase** or **ITP** (My rationale for this name is to set it apart from the roles these same transitional phrases may perform in other major sections of an essay). This ITP should come immediately after the attacking opening statement otherwise it will lead to clumsiness and confusion in your attack. The main function of this ITP in the explanation is to set up the major arguments in your introduction. Subsequent sentences in the introduction help to counter this argument before you round off the paragraph with your thesis statement.

ITPs THAT SET UP ARGUMENTS IN THE INTRODUCTION

1. In the first place...
2. On one hand...
3. To begin with...

4. For one thing…

Etc…

ITPs THAT COUNTER ARGUMENTS IN THE INTRODUCTION

1. On the other hand…
2. In spite of this…
3. Nevertheless
4. On the contrary…

Etc…

TRANSITIONS THAT BEGIN THE THESIS STATEMENT

1. It stands to reason therefore that…
2. Be that as it may…
3. In effect…
4. In spite of…
5. Despite…

To sum up, we can say that introductory transitional phrases (ITPs) allow you to write exciting introductions. First, an ITP helps you to **set up** one side of the argument, after the opening statement. Next, you **counter** this set-up with an opposite side argument, using another ITP. Finally, you round off both arguments with the **thesis**

statement, which is, in turn, introduced by a transition.

In effect, the **introduction** to an essay has **four components**:
1. The attacking opening statement (topic sentence)
2. The set-up argument
3. The counterargument
4. The thesis statement

It is actually easier than it sounds. Let me illustrate this with a few examples. The first example is taken from the essay on Immigration.

EXAMPLE 1.

Essay Question: *IS IMMIGRATION GOOD?*

OUTLINE

I. INTRODUCTION

Thesis Statement: Rather than being a negative phenomenon, immigration has been and continues to be a major force in nation-building because it has a lot benefits.

II. BODY

A. POSITIVES
  1. More taxes
  2. Increase in consumer demand
  3. Increase in productivity

B. NEGATIVES
 1. Deflating the job market with cheap labor

2. Increase in violence through gang activity
3. Drain on health care
   III. CONCLUSION

INTRODUCTION:

   It is very easy to describe immigration as very bad for a country. **For one thing**, the media has so often highlighted its negative aspects to the extent that it is always blamed for a country's economic woes. **On the other hand**, others see immigration as a very positive event and largely the reason why the United States of America has grown to become the greatest country in the world. *In spite of all the arguments and counter-arguments, however, immigration is a very powerful tool in nation-building because it provides a lot of benefits that lead to progress and development.*

   In Example 1, we can see all the four components of an introduction at play. The transitions are in italics with the ITPs in bold typeface:

1. The opening statement (topic sentence) with attack phrase: *It is very easy...*

2. The set-up argument with the ITP*: For one thing...*

3. The counterargument with an ITP: *On the other*

78

hand…

4. The thesis statement: *In spite of all the arguments…*

You will notice that the **thesis statement**, which is introduced by a transition, expresses an **opinion** on the **subject** or **topic under discussion** and it comes after we have briefly summarized the strongest arguments on both sides of the issue.

You will also notice that the thesis statement came up easily and logically from the set-up and the counter-argument elements of the introduction. Do not be surprised if—compared to how some English composition textbooks explain the thesis statement—this one seems too easy; there is no mystery to writing the thesis statement. All you need to do is to express your opinion on the subject under discussion.

This involves two steps:

1. You make a **claim** about the subject matter.

2. You give a **reason** or opinion on why your claim is true.

Example 1:

Thesis Statement: In spite of all the arguments and counter-arguments, however, immigration is a very powerful tool in nation-building because it provides a lot of benefits that lead to progress and development.

Claim: Immigration is a very powerful tool in nation-building…
Reason: …because it provides a lot of benefits that lead to progress and development.

Let us try writing another introduction using the four components above. This time, we will examine the issue of Drug Abuse.

EXAMPLE 2.
Essay Question:
"DRUG ABUSE CAN NEVER BE ERADICATED IN POOR NEIGHBORHOODS." Do you agree or disagree with this statement?
OUTLINE
I. INTRODUCTION
Thesis Statement: Drug abuse can be eradicated from poor neighborhoods because when the right measures and policies are put in place, it will eliminate all the negative influences.
II. BODY
A. CAUSES OF DRUG ABUSE IN POOR NEIGHBORHOODS
 1. Availability

2. Lax Security
3. Poor Government Policies

B. SOLUTIONS TO DRUG ABUSE IN POOR NEIGHBORHOODS
1. Strict Laws
2. Social Interventions
3. Sound Government Policies
III. CONCLUSION

INTRODUCTION

To state outright that drug abuse can never be eradicated in deprived neighborhoods is an extreme position. **Admittedly**, easy access to drugs and lax security in poor neighborhoods give drug pushers a free pass to carry on their business. **On the other hand**, studies have shown that great social intervention programs and stricter police patrols have been able to rid whole communities of this menace. *It stands to reason, therefore, that drug abuse in poor neighborhoods can be overcome because when the right measures are put in place, they'll eliminate the negative influences.*

In Example 2, we see all four elements of the introduction at play. The transitions are in italics and the ITPs are bold:

81

1. The opening statement (topic sentence) with attack phrase: *To state outright that...*
2. The set-up argument with the ITP: *On one hand...*
3. The counter-argument with the ITP: *On the other hand...*
4. The thesis statement: *It stands to reason, therefore, that...*

<u>Thesis Statement</u>: It stands to reason, therefore, that drug abuse in poor neighborhoods can be overcome because when the right measures are put in place, they will eliminate the negative influences.

Claim: Drug abuse in poor neighborhoods can be overcome...
Reason: ...because when the right measures are put in place, they will eliminate the negative influences.

This goes to illustrate further that there is no mystery about the thesis statement; you only have to apply these elements and the rest will follow logically.

*

DOES THIS "ATTACKING" APPROACH TO WRITING INTRODUCTIONS HAVE A BASIS IN ACADEMIC WRITING?

The answer is "Yes." First of all, it is based on Stephen Toulmin's mid-twentieth studies on the structure of the argument. According to Toulmin, an argument (i.e. thesis statement) should have a **Claim**, **Reason**, **Warrant** and **Evidence**. This implies that a thesis statement makes a claim which is supported by a reason. The two parts together-the claim and reason-lead us to the warrant, which is the writer's main argument or opinion. In other words, the warrant is the main idea the writer wants to persuade his audience to accept after reading his essay. This is supported by Wysocki and Lynch's observation that the warrant is "an idea or value that a writer believes the audience is likely to accept" (103).

Let me illustrate this with a thesis statement like this:

The Federal government should control healthcare because the states are not offering good health coverage for the poor.

Claim: The Federal government should take over health care.

Reason: The states are not giving good health coverage to the poor.

Warrant: The Federal government should have control over what affects the poor.

The rest of the essay will then be devoted to providing support or evidence for this thesis statement: the factors or reasons why the Federal government needs to take over health care delivery.

Secondly, the "Attacking" approach satisfies a very high requirement of academic argument—the concession. According to Mauk and Metz (242), there are four main elements in academic writing (i.e. the essay's introduction):

i. **Main claim or thesis**

ii. **Support**

iii. **Counterargument**

iv. **Concession**

Normally, the tendency in argumentative essays is to take a very strong position on your arguments. But this can turn off the very people you are trying to persuade. One way of winning them over is to make a **concession** to opposing arguments before hitting them with yours. This makes your arguments more mature. Thus, instead of a straight out argument, you end up having a "conversation with readers about an argumentative position" (Mauk and Metz 260).

Let us measure Mauk and Metz's requirements against an "Attacking" introduction:

To state outright that drug abuse can never be eradicated in deprived neighborhoods is an extreme position. **Admittedly, easy access to drugs and lax security in poor neighborhoods give drug pushers a free pass to carry on their business.** <u>On the other hand, studies have shown that great social intervention programs and stricter police patrols have been able to rid whole communities of this menace.</u> *It stands to reason, therefore, that drug abuse in poor neighborhoods can be overcome if the right measures are put in place.*

In the above example, I have used various devices to highlight the sections of the "attacking" introduction that meet Mauk and Metz's criteria for academic writing. The first sentence is the **main claim**. The sentence in bold typeface is both the **concession** and the **counterargument** (to the main claim). The underlined sentence is the **support** for the main claim and the italicized sentence constitutes the **thesis statement**.

This proves that our "attacking" introduction fulfils the requirements of academic writing: it has a <u>main claim</u>, <u>support</u>, <u>counterargument</u> and <u>concession</u>. By academic standards, therefore, the Arloo Matrix introduction works very well.

The second part of the introduction to an essay—which is normally continued in the next or second paragraph—is where you define the topic under discussion. For instance, if the essay prompt is about immigration, you will have to define immigration. If it is about dangerous driving, you will have to define it. And if the essay asks for features of democracy, you will have to define what democracy is.

One thing you should note is the distinction between an exam paper and a class assignment. In the exam situation, especially when you are writing an opinion essay, you cannot always summon a textbook or dictionary definition. Just define it to the best of your ability. The other elements of the matrix—the explanation and the evidence—will clarify it. In a class assignment, however, you have the time and resources to do so. Here are a couple of examples from the full-text essays in Appendix I and II:

Example 1 (Opinion Essay).
A character trait refers to certain habits and behaviors of an individual that tell you what type of person he or she is. **This makes it possible to**

predict how such a person is likely to behave in a particular situation. In other words, it gives us a hint into the person's underlying values and beliefs and how he or she lives his life and responds to the world. For example, when we describe a certain person as honest and hardworking or aggressive and lazy, we are describing that person's traits.

Example 2 (Academic Essay):

Domestic violence usually refers to the "use or threat of physical, sexual or emotional force by spouses, partners, relatives or anyone else with a close relationship with their victims" (Kearns et al. 12). **This implies that any act which has a harmful effect on any individual in the family can be described as domestic violence.** Such acts include insults, beatings, food deprivations, emotional abuse, forced labor and so on. It occurs in every sphere of society regardless of education, wealth, race and culture. It is caused by a lot of factors but some of the major ones are cheating, alcoholism, substance abuse, unemployment and poverty.

In the two examples of the definition paragraph shown above, the italicized sentences make up the topic sentences while the bold sentences constitute the explanation. The last sentences make up the evidence or support for the topic sentence.

What you need to remember about the definition, however, is that it is not necessary for every essay. It is very important in essays that evaluate a theory, a principle or a hot new topic, because your readers need to understand what you are talking about. But in most essays, especially opinion essays, you need not hang yourself about it since most people already know what you are talking about. You will need, however, to discuss it with your course lecturers to know their preferences.

OTHER WAYS OF STARTING INTRODUCTIONS

I want you to keep in mind that defining the essay topic is not the only way to begin your introductions. According to Kirszner and Mandell, depending on the subject or essay type, one way involves giving some background on your topic before stating your thesis or your position on the argument. Another way is to start with a short narrative or tell a little story by way of introducing your subject, followed by your thesis statement. Or you can simply begin with a quotation and take off from there (39).

John Mauk and John Metz also give similar advice. In addition to the anecdote, they recommend beginning your introduction with a provocative question or a shocking statement. But their most popular advice for beginning students, by far, is to begin with a sweeping statement about the nature of the debate. This serves the dual function of both teaching the reader about the topic and setting the tone for the debate (256).

There are no hard and fast rules. Only remember that you are writing with a certain purpose, which is to explain your thesis or opinion on the subject under discussion and to persuade your reader as to the soundness of your position. Your every paragraph and sentence should, therefore, be geared towards this purpose.

SUMMARY OF THE STANDARD (ARGUMENTATIVE) ESSAY'S MAIN POINTS

The first part of the book has dealt with the most important things to know about the principles of the Arloo Essay Matrix®. First, we tackled the introduction, with an emphasis on writing crisp, aggressive paragraphs and solid thesis statements that leave your reader or professor with no ambiguity about your position on the subject matter.

Under this section, we learned how to use an "attack phrase" to begin our opening statement. After that, we used introductory transitional phrases (ITPs) to begin our set-up and counterarguments. To complete our introduction, we introduced our thesis statements with transitions or transitional phrases.

Next, we touched on the body paragraphs, with special emphasis on the topic sentence, the explanation and the evidence. Every paragraph should have these elements for it to be considered "well-structured."

Finally, we studied the importance of the conclusion. We learned that it was the last word on the essay and, therefore, needed to be solid by reminding the reader of the essay's major arguments and its thesis statement.

Below is a chart showing the structure of your essay if you have followed all the principles in the matrix.

Chart 1: THE ARLOO ESSAY MATRIX

FOR THE STANDARD ESSAY

MAJOR SECTION OF ESSAY	PARAGRAPH ELEMENTS

INTRODUCTION	1. Opening statement (SI 1)
	2. Set-up argument (SI 2)
	3. Counterargument (SI 3)
	4. Thesis statement (SI 4)
BODY	1. Topic sentence (SB 1)
	2. Explanation (SB 2)
	3. Evidence (SB 3)
CONCLUSION	1. Summary of All Arguments (SC 1)
	2. Affirmation of

	Thesis Statement by Arguments (SC 2)

KEY:

S—Standard Essay

I—Introduction

B—Body

C—Conclusion

The numbers give you an idea of the number of sentences required in the paragraph.

As you can see from the chart above, essay writing can actually be reduced to the level of a **mathematical formula** or **matrix** from which countless essay structures can be created, both for the standard or narrative/descriptive essay formats, or a hybrid of both types. A hybrid essay is one that asks for both standard/argumentative and narrative/descriptive elements. These types of essays are usually found in college scholarship or admission essays. The questions are usually framed like this:

1. *Describe an important incident in your life. What impact did it make on the rest of your life?*

2. Tell us about a movie, song, book, or article that has inspired you. Why?

In order to create our matrix, we can have the following combinations:

1. **Standard Essay**= (SI1+ SI2 +SI3+SI4) + (SB1 + SB2 + SB3) + (SC1 + SC2 + SC3)

2. **Narrative Essay**= (NI1 + NI2 + NI3 + NI4) + (NB1 + NB2 + NB3) + (NC1 + NC2 + NC3)

3. **Hybrid Essay** = (SI1+ SI2 +SI3+SI4) + (NB1 + NB2 + NB3) + (SB1 + SB2 + SB3) + (SC1 + SC2 + SC3).

KEY
S: Standard essay
I: Introduction
B: Body
C: Conclusion
N: Narrative essay
I1: Introduction's opening statement
I2: Introduction's set-up argument
I3: Introduction's counterargument
I4: Introduction's thesis statement

B1: Body paragraph's topic sentence
B2: Body paragraph's explanation
B3: Body paragraph's example
C1: Conclusion paragraph's topic sentence
C2: Listing of essay's main arguments
C3: Reiteration of **thesis statement**

(**Note:** The structure of the matrix is always based on the core demand of the essay question).

In a nutshell, the Arloo Essay Matrix helps to structure your paragraphs. It gives form and structure to an infinite variety of essay questions. The upshot of this is to give you massive confidence to **break down** and tackle every standard or argumentative (and indeed every narrative/descriptive) essay with vim, vigor and determination. And that ingredient is the key to writing exceptional essays.

EXERCISES

1. Now I want you to try writing introductions for the three essays you have been working on. See if you can come up with good thesis statements. Remember to put in all four components and do not forget your attack phrases and ITPs:

   I. The opening statement

II. The set-up argument
III. The counterargument
IV. The thesis statement

2. Let us apply our knowledge on writing introductions to an actual introduction from a TIME Magazine article. Go to the magazine's website (www.time.com) and locate this article. See if you can identify the four components that make up the article's introduction:
Name of Article: "Obama vs. the Church"
Author: Rich Lowry
Date of Issue: February 20, 2012 (Vol 179, No. 7)
Page 20, paragraph 1.

The paragraph in question is from an article which examines the conflict between President Obama's Affordable Health Care Act and the Catholic Church on the issue of providing insurance coverage on contraception for the Church's employees. It does not look like a perfect example of the matrix but it is (and, as you master your matrix, you will learn to play around and manipulate its various components).

You will notice how the attacking opening statement is set up as a general introduction to the conflict. This is then followed by the set-up argument in the second sentence which mentions Obama as the aggressor. The counterargument lets us know how, previously, another powerful leader—King Henry VIII—won his fight with the Catholic Church (third and fourth sentences). Finally, the writer introduces his thesis statement with the transition ("but"): "But unlike Henry, Obama will almost certainly be forced to back down" (Richard Lowry 20).

You may look for other top-class magazines like Newsweek, Vanity Fair, The Economist, scientific journals, and the like to see if you can identify these components. You may also look up passages from your class textbooks. They will provide you with a wealth of practice.

3. Now complete all three essays you have been using as exercises. They should have all the main sections (i.e. introduction, body and conclusion). Within each section, you must have the elements or components that meet all the requirements of the Arloo Essay Matrix Chart. Compare your essays to the chart and check off the following:

I. Introduction: SI 1

SI 2

SI 3

SI 4

II. Body: SB 1

SB 2

SB 3 (Note: Each Body paragraph must have an SB1, SB2, and SB3)

III. Conclusion: SC 1

SC 2

SC 3 (Depends on the academic level of the student).

PART TWO: THE NARRATIVE ESSAY

CHAPTER 7

THE NARRATIVE ESSAY—A DEFINITION

Everybody loves stories. From news items to talent shows like "American Idol" or "The X-Factor," I have seen hosts and audiences alike moved more by contestants' personal stories than any obvious talents. Who can ever forget 2005 American Idol winner Fantasia Barrino or double-amputee Oscar "Blade Runner" Pistorius at the 2012 London Olympics?

Growing up in Ghana, I remember a childhood spent by the fireside on moonlit nights when my grandmother would hold us spellbound with stories about Kweku Ananse, the wily spider who got so good at outwitting people, he even tried to trick God. And on other days, my mother would regale us with stories from movies she had seen, stories about good and bad witches who terrorized our dreams long before I discovered Grimm's fairy tales in our local library.

Around age nine, I discovered a little book in the library called "Aesop's Fables". It had fantastic stories about animals trying to outsmart each other. But the difference between Aesop's fables and other fairy tales was that at the end of every fable, it restated the moral or lesson taught by the story. In this respect, Aesop's fables are like the narrative essays you will be asked to write in your high school, GED, college freshman English classes, Title III scholarship or GRE; you will have to state any lessons you learned from your experiences or narratives.

DEFINITION:

A NARRATIVE ESSAY is one that asks you to tell a story—usually about something that happened to you—and the lessons you learned from that experience. In other words, the narrative essays you write will ask you to narrate an important or significant event in your life, the lessons you learned from that particular incident or experience, and how it has contributed to who you are today. Thus, you might be asked to write about your first trip outside your country, for example. Or your first day at school. The list is endless.

THE STRUCTURE OF THE NARRATIVE ESSAY

There are a lot of ways to lay out the outline or structure of the narrative essay. For me, however, one of the most effective ways is to use the Five –

Question Template. I am referring to the "Who?", "When?", "Where?", "What?", and "Why?" questions which have been used all over the world to lay out the standard outline of journalistic reporting or the narrative essay. Whoever came up with this template has done students—and indeed, every writer—a world of good. The reason is that it:

1. Conforms to the basic structure of every essay: the introduction, the body and the conclusion.

2. Lays out the main phases of every narrative or descriptive essay; the beginning, the middle, and the end.

3. Helps readers follow the chronological order or dramatic sequence in which the narrative's events take place.

4. Makes it easier for the student to keep track of verb tenses, which are crucial to every narrative essay. Failure to do so will lead to shifts in verb tense, a recipe for confusion.

In effect, therefore, these questions allow your readers to experience the people, places, time, the intense emotions and the lessons that make up your story or narrative.

THE FIVE - QUESTION TEMPLATE

1. "WHO?" This question refers to the **central character** or **protagonist** involved in the narrative.

Depending on the type of essay question or prompt, you may be asked to write about your own experiences or that of someone close to you. You may also be asked to write about a historical figure or event. The "Who?" segment helps you to introduce the main character or protagonist. For example, you may be asked to write about the biggest disappointment of your life. With an essay prompt like this, you become the "Who" or the protagonist. This question helps you to immediately focus on the events in your own life. On the other hand, you may be asked to write about, for instance, the events that led to the Rodney King Riots in Los Angeles in 1993. In this case, Rodney King becomes the protagonist.

Another function of this segment is to provide biographical details of the protagonist in the narrative, answering questions like name, age, profession, nationality, and so on.

2. "WHEN?" Every event occurs in a specific time frame and place. But this "When" is about more than a date. It talks about the occasion or special event and the incidents or actions that might have led to it. It also talks about the mood and ambience of the event. The end result is a paragraph rich in detail, easily conjuring a specific atmosphere for the

reader. For instance, an event which takes place at Christmas obviously has its own ambience, as compared to an event taking place in mid-summer or during the spring-break.

3. "WHERE?" Like the "When?" question, this one describes the specific location or place where the event or events took place. It also helps you to fill in details about the location, conjuring more specific sights, sounds and smells which help to color and provide a mood for the event. In effect, this question makes it easy for you to describe the location in specific detail for the reader and, and for the more creative student, put in some creative effects like foreshadowing, symbolism, and other literary devices.

4. "WHAT?" This is actually the **CORE DEMAND**, or most important part of the narrative essay. Whether your essay will be boring or exciting depends on the effort you put into this segment. This part of the essay allows you to tell your readers about the climactic act or incident that is at the core of your essay. For this reason, I normally encourage students to use about three paragraphs in this segment:

Paragraph 1: The **beginning** of the climactic act or event.

Paragraph 2: The **middle** of the climactic act or event.

Paragraph 3: The end or **climax** of the climactic act or event.

5. "WHY?" This question signals the **denouement** or **end** of the narration. It performs a role identical to that of the conclusion in a persuasive or argumentative essay. This final part talks about lessons learned from the event or incident. It summarizes the impressions and life-lessons you must have learnt or taken away from that particular experience. It also helps you to write a fitting conclusion to your narrative essay by listing key points or events and restating how they support your thesis which was laid out in the introduction.

To sum up, the Five-Question Template shows that, like the argumentative and other essays, the narrative or descriptive essay has an **introduction** which introduces the subject and thesis statement. It also has a **body** ("Who?", "When?", "Where?" and "What?") which lays out the events of the narrative sequentially and clearly.

Lastly, it ends with a **conclusion** ("Why?") which restates the thesis and reinforces it by summarizing the key incidents or events in the narrative and their lasting impression on the protagonist.

A typical narrative essay's outline will, therefore, look like this:

I. INTRODUCTION

Thesis Statement

II. BODY
1. Who?
2. When?
3. Where?
4. What?

III. CONCLUSION

Why?

We will discuss this outline in greater detail later.

EXERCISES

1. Go online and select three narrative, and one descriptive essay topic.

2. Write complete outlines for your chosen topics, using the Five-Question Template.

CHAPTER 8

The Arloo Essay Matrix Vs The Narrative Essay

Does the Arloo Essay Matrix apply to a narrative essay whose emphasis is on narration rather than argument?

The answer is "YES." Let me explain.

You will remember the **core elements** of the Arloo Matrix, as they relate to paragraph structure, are:

1. The topic sentence.
2. The explanation.
3. The example.

In the argumentative essay, the topic sentence states the main point of the paragraph. This is then supported by the explanation, comprising two-to-five or more sentences that break down and explain the topic sentence. The final component is the evidence, which is cited to support the main point or topic sentence.

Similarly, in the case of the narrative essay, the topic sentence remains the **key** or **primary** sentence. But instead of expressing a main point or argument, it provides a direct answer to one of the five questions in the template. In short, the topic sentence directly answers either the "Who," "When," "Where," "What," or "Why" questions.

The explanation component of the paragraph also transforms into the details or descriptions which flesh out and expand the key or primary sentence (i.e. the direct answer to the template question).

The evidence, which normally rounds up the argumentative paragraph, becomes transformed into the writer or student's feelings about that particular paragraph, phase or sequence in the narration. In effect, where the last component in an argumentative or standard essay's body paragraph would have been evidence or support to buttress the topic sentence, the last sentence in a narrative body paragraph expresses the writer's impressions or feelings about that particular phase of the event or incident.

As illustrated in the first part of this book with the standard essay (pages 90-1), I have also provided a chart to explain the dynamics of the Arloo Essay Matrix and the structure of the narrative/descriptive essay.

Chart 2: The Arloo Essay Matrix for the

Narrative Essay

MAJOR SECTION OF ESSAY	PARAGRAPH ELEMENTS
INTRODUCTION	1.Attacking opening statement (NI 1) 2. Set-up argument (NI 2) 3. Counterargument (NI 3) 4. Thesis statement (NI 4)
BODY	(The Five-Question Template) 1. Direct answer to template question (NB

	1)
	2.
	Narrative/descriptive detail (NB 2)
	3. Feelings or impressions (NB 3)
CONCLUSION	1. Summary of all key incidents (NC 1)
	2. Affirmation of thesis statement by key incidents (NC 2)

KEY:
N—Narrative/descriptive essay
I—Introduction
Body—Body
C—Conclusion

Let me illustrate how the Arloo Matrix works in the standard and narrative essays by comparing the following paragraphs. Paragraphs 1 and 3 are from a standard (opinion) essay while 2 and 4 are taken from a narrative essay.

1. Standard Essay

Secondly, my persistence has influenced my life in school. **I am not the brightest student in class. But whenever I am given a class assignment, I start work on it the same day. I make sure I get the necessary books and follow the instructions carefully. And I always turn my work in on time. Because of this my teachers always praise me and tell others to follow my example.** In my last year in Junior high school, for instance, I got an award for always turning my work in before everybody else.

2. Narrative Essay

The city was bustling with activity when I arrived. **Since it was the peak of the tourism season, a lot of activities were lined up; traditional festivals, theater and street jams. There were long lines of cars, taxis and trucks caught in traffic jams. Impatient drivers tooted their horns at aggressive food vendors and petty**

traders jostling for space. The few policemen trying to maintain order were ineffective. And everybody was sweating from their efforts. It was mayhem.

In Paragraph 1, the main idea or key sentence is in italics. When you compare it to the first sentence in Paragraph 2 (which is also in italics), you will notice they are both stating the main idea in their respective paragraphs. Thus, both sentences conform to the topic sentence in the matrix. Similarly, the sentences appearing in bold type in Paragraph 2 perform the role of the explanation in the standard essay paragraph (Paragraph 1); it fleshes out and expands the main idea in the topic sentence by adding detail. In that respect, the narrative/descriptive detail segment of the narrative essay's body paragraph is equivalent to the explanation in the standard essay.

The last similarity between the standard essay's body paragraph and that of the narrative body paragraph is found in the last sentences of both examples. In the standard paragraph, the last sentence gives evidence to support the key sentence. Similarly, in the narrative paragraph, the last sentence gives the writer's impressions on the main idea in the key sentence. Thus, both sentences are performing the same role here, which is to round off the paragraph by supporting the main idea.

Examine Paragraphs 3 and 4 closely to see if you can break them down into their components, as we did with Paragraphs 1 and 2.

3. Standard Essay

Domestic violence has caused and continues to create a lot of social problems. *But some of the most devastating of these effects are loss of lives and permanent disability sustained by its victims.* **This implies that the violence between intimate partners and among family members causes a lot of harm and suffering to both victims and perpetrators. Citing studies by Boursnell and Prosser (2010), Lynda Gibbons observes that a lot of domestic attacks involves "slapping, kicking, hitting, punching, burning or scalding, use of weapons or destruction of property; it often results in injury and can lead to death" (12).** According to Gibbons, in the UK the Home Office reported that of all the murder cases reported in 2011, 76% of women and 50% of men were killed by people known to the victims (12).

4. Narrative Essay

In July of 2005, I was working as a TV producer at McCann-Eriksson, one of the top advertizing agencies in Accra, the capital of Ghana. **Because of the noise in the capital, however, I lived in Tema, which was about twenty miles away and much quieter. It had been a hectic year with lots of TV commercials so when my vacation time came, I grabbed it with enthusiasm. After a week at home in Tema, I decided to travel to my hometown to have a great reunion with my cousins and uncles. But before leaving, I had to pick up a check from my office.** It was with a lot of anticipation that I drove to Accra.

EXERCISES

From the outlines you have developed on your selected essay topics at the end of Chapter 7, write three body paragraphs for each topic.

CHAPTER 9

The Narrative Essay–The Introduction

Every essay has an introduction which introduces the subject and lays out the writer's thesis statement. And the narrative essay is no different. But while the standard argumentative essay's introduction introduces the topic and states the thesis, the narrative introduction introduces the main character or protagonist in the story. Here too, the thesis statement is nothing more than your opinion on the event(s) in the narration. In other words, you have to state whether you were positively or negatively affected by the event(s). Then, just as we did with the argumentative essay, the rest of the essay goes to lend support to—or prove—your thesis.

You will remember that when we worked on the introduction for the argumentative essay, we identified a series of devices to help us set up the thesis statement. These were:

The Four Components of an Introduction

1. The attacking opening statement (topic sentence)

2. The set-up argument
3. The counterargument
4. The thesis statement

In the narrative essay, these elements work in an identical fashion. First, **a general statement or definition** is made about the essay topic in relation to the **protagonist**. This is similar to the attacking opening statement in an argumentative essay. Then an ITP (introductory transitional phrase) leads you to **set up** one side of the argument. Next, you bring in the **counterargument** with the help of another ITP. Here, you state an opposing argument or what could have been an **opposite** outcome of the narrative. Finally, you finish it off with the **thesis statement**, which is, in turn, introduced by a transition. Let us see how it works, using two fictional narrative essays. The first one is titled "My Deepest Regret." The second essay topic is "An Important Lesson I Learned."(The complete essays for both topics are in Appendix II). Both outlines are provided below.

NARRATIVE ESSAY 1: My Deepest Regret
OUTLINE
I. INTRODUCTION

<u>Thesis Statement</u>: I failed to take advantage of a glorious opportunity and I have regretted it since and also learned to never procrastinate.

II. BODY
- A. Who? : Some autobiographical details about myself.
- B. When? : The occasion was during my annual vacation when I went to Accra to pick up my check at the office.
- C. Where? : The incident took place in Accra during a visit to my friend's office.
- D. What? : Meeting world-famous musician, Billy Ocean.
  1. Beginning: Seeing him in the parking lot and failing to recognize him.
  2. Middle: Learning at Eric's office that it was actually Billy Ocean
  3. End: The frantic search for Billy Ocean.

III. CONCLUSION
- E.   Why?
  - A. Summary of main incidents
  - B. Reinforcement/affirmation of thesis on important lesson learned:
  "Never fail to take advantage of an opportunity. When unsure, ask for help."

NARRATIVE ESSAY 2: An Important Lesson I Learned

OUTLINE

I. INTRODUCTION

Thesis Statement: If I had not been too quick to dismiss someone due to his scruffy appearance, I would have landed the most lucrative job in my life.

II. BODY

 A. Who? : A few autobiographical details about myself.

   B. When? : The occasion was after graduation from college with my Bachelor's degree and getting an invitation to an interview.

   C. Where? : The visit to the Coca Cola Headquarters.

   D. What? : The interview

     1. Beginning: Preparations for the interview – meeting the scruffy beggar.

     2. Middle: At the interview.

     3. End: The revelation of the board chairman's identity.

III. CONLUSION

     Why?

     A. Summary of main incidents

     B. Reinforcement/affirmation of thesis on important lesson learned:

"Never judge people by their appearance."

You will notice that when followed faithfully, the Five-Question template makes it easy to plan your outline. It also gives your essay a solid structure so that, in the event that you get carried away by the beauty of your own brilliant story, you can find your way safely back.

EXAMPLE 1:
My Deepest Regret
INTRODUCTION

Most people, when asked about their deepest regret in life, will tell you they do not have any. *For one thing*, it is probably the most embarrassing or painful incident in their lives and best forgotten. *On the other hand*, most people would rather not admit it since it will make you lose respect for them. For me, however, the answer is simple. *There is one incident that causes me a lot of pain and regret whenever I think about it. And it is not something I did. Rather, it is something I failed to do and it taught me to never procrastinate.*

118

In the above introduction the main components are in italics. We begin with the **opening statement** which introduces the topic, "My Deepest Regret." We continue by **setting up** one side of the argument using an **ITP**. Next, we bring in the **counterargument** using another ITP. We then finish the paragraph by making our thesis statement, which also introduces the **protagonist** or **main character** ("Who?") in the story (me).

Let us try another one, this time on the essay topic: "An Important Lesson I learned" (The complete essay can be found in Appendix II).

EXAMPLE 2:

An Important Lesson I learned
INTRODUCTION

To say that life is all about the lessons we learn is to make it seem too simple. *On one hand,* we do not have to read deep meanings into every little incident that takes place in our lives; that would rob us of life's lighter moments. *On the other hand,* we cannot ignore the lessons that life teaches us to help solve future problems in our lives. *Be that as it may, one of the most important lessons I learned in life was that I should never judge people based on their appearance.*

In the above example, we begin the attack with a general observation about the topic of life's lessons. Then, using an ITP, we set up the first argument about life's lessons. Next, we counter with an opposing argument using another ITP. Finally, using a transition, we finish off with our thesis statement, which also introduces the protagonist ("Who?") in the narrative, which happens to be me.

EXERCISES

1. Think of some significant events in your life and the impact(s) they made on your development.

2. Select two of these events to use as your assignments. Beginning from the next Chapter (10), set out these events in a narrative essay outline and apply all the principles you will learn from each chapter into writing two complete narrative essays. This will give you a priceless hands-on experience with the Arloo Matrix as it applies to the narrative essay.

3. Write two introductions for the topics you have chosen to write about.

CHAPTER 10

The Narrative–The Body Paragraph

Now let us take a look at how to develop our body paragraphs using the body template questions—Who? When, Where? and What? The examples have been taken from the two essays whose outlines were discussed in the previous chapter (Chapter 9). Example #1 always refers to the essay topic "My Deepest Regret" and Example #2 refers to "An Important Lesson I learned."

1. THE "WHO?"

This question introduces the segment where we fill out the biographical details of the protagonist. We get to know how things like his or her age, personality, profession, likes and dislikes have a bearing on the narrative. This helps to fill out the main character so that it does not appear as if we are writing about an invisible being. In short, this question or segment brings our protagonist to life.

Let me illustrate this point using our fictional essays.

EXAMPLE 1:

Billy Ocean is one of the most celebrated musicians in the world. He is a British musician whose peak years were in the late 1980s and 1990s.He had a lot of hit songs but some of the most popular are "Caribbean Queen," "Suddenly," "Get out of My Car," "When The Going Gets Tough," and "Stay the Night." In high school, no dance came to life till his song "Caribbean Queen" was played. Indeed, I was so crazy about his music I was nick-named "Billy Ocean."

EXAMPLE 2:

My name is Kofi Annan and the last of four children born to my parents. The others are girls. The first born, Amanda, is a doctor at the Teaching Hospital. The next one, Esi, is a successful lawyer and the last girl is Afua, a very successful businesswoman with three shops in London. As you can see, my sisters' successes put an enormous pressure on me to excel in school which I did. And even though people said I was arrogant, I did not mind. After all, why should I lower my standards when it was not my fault I was so smart. I felt good about myself.

2. THE "WHEN?"

This segment deals with the date or occasion of the event. As mentioned earlier, every event occurs within a specific time frame. It can take place in a day, a few hours or even weeks. What you have to remember is that your essay is probably not going to be too long so it is better to limit your event to a day or two. The "When?" also refers to the occasion and the mood and ambience surrounding it. These sensory details add atmosphere and color to your descriptions and create specific feelings in your reader. For example, an event that takes place around Christmas has a mood very different from an event in summer. Similarly, your first job interview will probably be different from a graduation party. And, at the end of the paragraph, do not forget to add your special feelings or impressions.

A couple of examples will help here.

EXAMPLE 1.

In July of 2005, I was working as a TV producer at McCann-Eriksson, one of the top advertizing agencies in Accra, the capital of Ghana. Because of the noise in the capital, however, I lived in Tema, which was about twenty miles away and much quieter. It had been a hectic year shooting lots of TV commercials so when my vacation time came, I grabbed it with enthusiasm. After a week at home in Tema, I decided to travel to my hometown—which was about two hundred miles away—to have a great reunion with my cousins and uncles. But before leaving, I had to pick up a check from my office. It was with a lot of anticipation that I drove to Accra.

EXAMPLE 2.

I had just graduated from college with a degree in Business Administration and, after sending out hundreds of applications, I got a letter from the Coca-Cola Company to attend an interview at their headquarters on the 13th of June, 2010. It was the biggest company in my country and, as a child, I used to dream about working there. For one thing, the salary was great and it came with a lot of perks, not to mention the prestige. As I lay in bed the night before the interview, I offered a prayer of thanks to God for the chance to work there. It was an awesome opportunity.

3. THE "WHERE?"

This question introduces the segment on the location or place where the event took place. The problem with this segment is that most students gloss over or skip this segment in a sentence or two, rendering their essays colorless and weak. Big mistake. For your essay to look authentic, you will have to fill in a lot of descriptive detail about where the event takes place. For instance, you will have to create or provide details about the geography of the location, whether it is a hilly or low-lying area, a big city or small town, coastal or countryside. Details about the kind of people you will meet there also help. So do descriptions of the buildings. The bottom line is to paint a picture for your reader to see the location clearly in his mind.

The danger here is to offer too much descriptive detail. Remember, your essay is probably limited by time or length or both. Two to four sentences of description would do. And do not forget to add your impressions at the very end of the paragraph.

Let us look at a couple of examples.

EXAMPLE 1.

The city was bustling with activity when I arrived. Since it was the peak of the tourism season, a lot of activities were lined up: traditional festivals, theater and street jams. There were long lines of cars, taxis and trucks caught up in traffic. Impatient drivers tooted their horns at aggressive food vendors and petty traders jostling for space. The few policemen trying to maintain order were ineffective. And everybody was sweating from their efforts. It was mayhem.

EXAMPLE 2.

The Coca-Cola Head Office was located at the end of Spintex Road, an area specially set aside for the biggest corporations in Ghana. The buildings were very tall and mostly made of chrome and glass. The tallest among them, almost fifty storeys high, had the Coca-Cola logo embossed on it in huge steel letters. Shady trees lined the car park where well-built uniformed guards strolled about with batons in their belt. It was a really intimidating place.

4. THE "WHAT?"

This is the most important part of your essay, the core demand. It is the climax of the story. If your narration here is dull and unexciting, you will fail to impress the reader. The reason is that this segment is where you convince the reader about what is so special about the event or incident that it had such a lasting impact on your life. In short, you need to pay particular attention to this section. I am not saying you should be overdramatic or go overboard. Just make sure your narration has a ring of authenticity to it.

Also, as mentioned earlier, this segment is so crucial that you will do well to split it into three: the beginning, the middle and the end. The first

126

paragraph describes what happens at the beginning of the climatic event, the second describes the action in the middle and the end describes the final act.

Let us study our examples.

EXAMPLE 1.

<u>Beginning of Climax</u>

I decided to call on Eric, one of my high schoolmates. His office was located in a high-rise along my route. The car park was crowded with lots of smartly-dressed people lounging around. I saw someone who resembled Billy Ocean leaning against one car. I nodded by way of greeting and he responded with a smile and a nod. The resemblance was uncanny but I did not pay any attention to it. What would Billy Ocean be looking for in a small country like Ghana on a weekday? Besides there had been no news report that he was in town. When I got to my friend's office, he was bubbling over. When he had calmed down a bit, he gave me the reason for his excitement: Billy Ocean had just walked out of his office after signing a deal to perform in Ghana later in the year. Billy Ocean himself! I could have kicked myself till I bled.

<u>Middle of Climax</u>

I rushed downstairs with my friend so that he would introduce me. But what I actually wanted was a photograph with him. It was a chance of a lifetime! Panting and sweating, we raced into the parking lot. But it was empty. All the cars had left. The only person left in the car park was the security guard who was smiling at an autographed CD in his hand. It was Billy Ocean's "Caribbean Queen"! I asked him where Billy Ocean was. All he told me was "They've left." It almost made me cry.

End of Climax

Eric tried to console me with the fact that I could get to see him in a few months but I would not be comforted. We tried calling Billy's manager to locate him so I could meet and take a photograph with him but no one picked his call. He kept trying till his battery went dead. I left Eric in the car park but not before extracting a firm promise from him on a ticket to Billy's show. I was beyond heartbroken.

EXAMPLE 2.
Beginning of Climax

Just before I entered the building, I was approached by a scruffy-looking man with a tribal mark on his left cheek. He wanted some money for food since he hadn't eaten for three days. I was already tense because of the interview so I ignored him. When he tried to hold my arm, I shoved him off. He fell into the flower bed. I almost followed up with a kick. How dare him!

Middle of Climax

When I arrived at the Conference Room, where the interview was being held, I met four other candidates. They appeared more nervous than me but we smiled at each other. Then I was ushered into a smaller office where two distinguished-looking gentlemen interviewed me. I was smart and confident with my answers and one of them commended me on the excellence of my diction. I even managed to get them to laugh a couple of times. It could not have gone better.

End of Climax

As we got to the end of the interview, a door to the side of the office opened and a man in an expensive suit entered, his back facing us as he closed the door. My interviewers rose so I did the same. Then the man turned and faced us, smiling, a tribal mark on his left cheek. I froze—it was the scruffy man I had shoved into the flowerbed! He briefly explained that the incident downstairs was part of the interview process. Since Coca-Cola did a lot of charity work, they were looking for candidates with humanity. Obviously, he added, I had failed in that respect even though I was the smartest candidate. He wished me luck in my job search. Picking up my bag, I left the office, the tears running down my cheeks. What a fool I had been!

EXERCISES

Go back to the two essays you are working on. Write body paragraphs for each of them, using the questions Who? When? Where? and What? Be as creative as possible while remaining authentic.

CHAPTER 11

THE NARRATIVE ESSAY–THE CONCLUSION

5. THE 'WHY?"

This question performs a role identical to that of the conclusion in a standard or argumentative essay. This final part talks about lessons learned from the event or incident. It summarizes the impressions and life–lessons you must have learned or taken away from that particular experience. It helps you to write a fitting conclusion to your narrative essay by listing key points or events and restating how they support your thesis statement.

It also brings a final curtain on your essay. Remember, the narrative essay is always about some life lessons learned from the major event or incident in the narrative. Sometimes, when the narration is powerful and convincing, you may not even have to list the key incidents. Your final impressions will do just fine. Just keep it in mind that your impressions should not be overdramatized. A few, well-placed observations will do.

Let us look at our examples.

EXAMPLE 1.

As I drove to my office, I thought about the missed opportunity, an opportunity we had dreamed of since high school. Luckily for Eric, he had fulfilled his. I knew I would probably regret this for the rest of my life. But I had learned my lesson very well. Next time I was in a situation like that, where I was not too sure about something, I would go up and ask for clarification. I would never procrastinate again in my life.

You can, therefore, imagine my shock when I got to the office to discover that Billy Ocean and his manager had been to my office to sign the advertizing contract and Billy had taken pictures with everybody in the office. And I mean everybody! When I saw the photographs, it was all I could do not to collapse in pain!

EXAMPLE 2.

When I left the Coca-Cola building, I could not go home. I went to the beach and sat there for a long time, thinking about life and how we live it. I thought about how those to whom much is given must show kindness to the less privileged. I thought about my arrogance and impatience with people I considered inferior. Finally, I decided that from that moment on, I was going to be the kindest person in the world!

THE NARRATIVE ESSAY—PROBLEMS

Kirszner and Mandell made a number of observations concerning the main problems one encounters writing the narrative essay. Although these comments do not cover the entire scope of issues associated with the narrative essay, they are among the most important ones to watch out for (71).

1. Chronological Order: The most effective way to write the narrative essay is to lay out the events or incidents in the sequence in which they took place. This avoids confusion and helps you to focus on the narrative rather than some gimmicks to drive home your thesis.

2. Verb Tenses: This is important because you need to show the relationships between the times the events or incidents occurred. Thus, if you begin your essay with a particular tense (e.g. past), you should stick to that for the entire essay. If you have to use flash-back or flash-forward, carefully signal the shift in time by the appropriate transition and tense.

3. Transitions: Transitions in narrative essays perform the same roles they did in the standard

essays; they link paragraphs together. In addition, they help to link the events smoothly, helping the reader to understand and follow the correct order or sequence of events without losing thread of the narrative.

<u>Some effective Transitions in Narrative essays</u>

In the beginning...

First...

Second...

Next...

Then...

Later...

Immediately...

Before...

Soon...

In addition...

Meanwhile...

Afterwards...

Simultaneously...

At the same time...

Now...

Finally...

Eventually...

4. <u>Detail</u>: As every raconteur will tell you, "the devil is in the details". This simply means, for a story to be very convincing, there should be lots of details. This gives the narrative authenticity.

Hence, you would do well to describe the sights, sounds, smells and feelings in your narrative. If possible, you should provide the dates, times and locations of the events. Look at the sample essays in Appendix II to see how this is done.

EXERCISES

Go back to the two narrative essays you are working on and write the conclusions. Make sure to include the life-lessons you learned from the events or incidents. Be creative!

CHAPTER 12

OVERVIEW OF THE ARLOO ESSAY MATRIX ®

At this point it is reasonably safe to say that you have understood the basic principles of the Arloo Essay Matrix and how they work in college essay writing. Specifically, you can now tell the difference between the standard or argumentative essay (and similar such essays) on one hand, and the narrative or descriptive essay on the other.

Within the standard essay, you can tell the difference between an opinion essay and an academic essay or class paper. Within the narrative essay too, you can make reasonable adjustments if the essay prompt is emphasizing the narrative elements over the descriptive or vice versa, as happens when the essay is describing a process.

It is also important to remember that in the normal scheme of things, the logical and correct order of the major sections of the essay outline is:
I. Introduction
II. Body
III. Conclusion

But, you may have noticed that in this book, I started out teaching how to write the body paragraphs before touching on the conclusion and the introduction in that order. The reason I started this way was to teach you the simplicity of the writing process and have you develop confidence in writing great paragraphs. Once this confidence was established, it became easier to handle the more difficult aspects of the essay like the introduction and the conclusion.

So what have we learned about the Arloo Essay Matrix® process?

Let us look at it step-by-step.

I. THE INTRODUCTION:

We have learned that, whether it is argumentative or narrative, an essay's introduction is one of the most important sections and that the key to a great introduction rests on four important components:

A. The attacking opening statement
B. The set-up argument
C. The counterargument
D. The thesis statement

The **opening statement** tackles the question or essay topic aggressively. By attacking the question, you give yourself the upper-hand in steering and controlling the essay in any direction of your choice. This "attacking" opening statement is introduced by what we call the **"attack phrase,"** a special kind of transition which helps you open your essay in the strongest possible terms. Examples of these "attack phrases" are "It is easy to...," "To state outright that...," "It is very tempting to describe..." and so on.

Apart from the opening statement, the other three elements of the introduction also use what I call the **introductory transitional phrases** (ITPs). Examples of these are: "On one hand," "In the first place," and the like. The **set-up argument**, helped by the ITP, introduces one point-of-view or one side of the issue you are arguing on. The **counterargument**, also helped by an ITP, raises the other side of the issue or argument. When both of these arguments have been raised to highlight the main opposing issues on the essay topic, you finish both arguments off with the **thesis statement**, which is, in turn, introduced by a **transition**.

Following these steps will help you to write a catchy, interesting introduction that will capture the scope of your essay topic and finish it off with a solid thesis statement that leaves no doubts at all in the mind of your readers about the purpose of your essay.

We also learned that for these four elements to work, you need to know your transitions by heart so that you can use them effectively. Some of these transitions are: "Firstly," "Secondly," "Next," "Furthermore," "Lastly" and so on (Look up the complete list in Chapter 2, read other essay books, or go online).

II. THE BODY

We also established that the essay's body is crucial because this is where we set out and argue our main points in support of the thesis statement set forth in the introduction. This holds true for both the argumentative and narrative types. To help us perform this task, we touched on specific elements that would help us to lay out our arguments clearly and logically. These elements are the:

A. Topic sentence
B. Explanation
C. Evidence

Briefly, the **topic sentence** typically states the main idea in the paragraph. The **explanation** breaks it down and explains it. With the help of **sequential transitions**, this element uses **deductive reasoning** to expand the paragraph and provide more detail, thus developing logical coherent thought. The last element—the **evidence**—provides solid authoritative and other evidence to support the main idea set forth in the topic sentence.

Based on a chart of the matrix, we were able to point out that the elements of the paragraph were similar for both the argumentative and narrative essays.

Here too, an effective use of transitions will help to link your arguments and your paragraphs effortlessly, giving them logic and coherence. These transitions, particularly the ones that signal a contrast or change in the direction of flow, such as ""Nevertheless," "However," "In spite of," and the like, are priceless in shifting your arguments and points-of-view in your essay. In the case of the narrative type, transitions like 'Next," "Meanwhile," "Simultaneously," "Eventually," and so on, can be very useful. You would do well to master them.

III. THE CONCLUSION

The conclusion of the essay is as important as the introduction and the body because this is where you make your closing arguments. It is also your last paragraph and it leaves a lasting impression. So make it count.

The main elements in the conclusion, whether it is argumentative or narrative, are:

A. Summarize your arguments or main incidents.

B. Affirm your arguments and position, or lessons learned, according to your thesis statement.

Begin by summarizing all your arguments (i.e. the topic sentences of your body paragraphs). You can simply list them in a straightforward manner so that you do not confuse your reader. After that you re-state your thesis. The last thing you do is to state how your arguments bear out or support your thesis statement.

Here too, you must use your transitions effectively so that your arguments show coherence and logic. It is best to list all the supporting arguments on one side first, using incremental transitions like "Firstly," "Second," "Lastly," and so on. Next, you signal a shift in your arguments to the other side of the topic using contrast transitions like "However," "Nevertheless" and the like. Then you list all the counterarguments, again using incremental transitions like "First," "Furthermore," "In addition," and so on. After this, you end by evaluating your thesis statement, using closing transitions like "Be that as it may," "The bottom line," "It stands to reason," and the like.

APPLICATION OF THE ARLOO ESSAY MATRIX®

The next thing we will do is apply all we have learned in this little book to write a short standard essay (opinion type). We will follow the process from top to bottom, illustrating how it works. First, we will begin with the essay topic or prompt and write out the formal outline. This will be followed by the introduction, body and conclusion.

But before we write our standard essay, I want to hammer home the similarities between the standard and the narrative essay in terms of how they apply the Arloo Essay Matrix. Even though one essay type deals with argumentation and the other deals with narration/description, both use the same elements in their paragraphs. In other words, if you compare—for instance—the introduction in a standard essay to the introduction in a narrative, you will find that both have the same components:

A. An opening statement (i.e. attack)

B. Set-up argument

C. Counterargument

D. Thesis statement

The same similarities can be found in both the body paragraphs and the conclusions for both kinds of essays, as depicted in Charts 3 and 4 presented below.

Chart 3: Abridged Version of the Arloo

Essay Matrix® for the Standard Essay

MAJOR SECTION OF ESSAY	PARAGRAPH ELEMENTS
INTRODUCTION	1. Attacking opening statement 2. Set-up argument 3. Counterargument 4. Thesis statement
BODY	1. Topic sentence 2. Explanation 3. Evidence
CONCLUSION	1. Summary of all

	arguments
	2. Affirmation of thesis statement by arguments

C Chart 4: The Arloo Essay Matrix for the Narrative Essay

MAJOR SECTION OF ESSAY	PARAGRAPH ELEMENTS
INTRODUCTION	1.Attacking opening statement (NI 1) 2. Set-up argument (NI 2) 3. Counterargument

	(NI 3) 4. Thesis statement (NI 4)
BODY	(The Five-Question Template) 1. Direct answer to template question (NB 1) 2. Narrative/descriptive detail (NB 2) 3. Feelings or impressions (NB 3)
CONCLUSION	1. Summary of all key incidents (NC 1)

	2. Affirmation of thesis statement by key incidents (NC 2)

ESSAY PROMPT:

What do you consider to be the single most important societal problem? Why?

What is this prompt asking for? What are the **core demands** of the question? You will remember that in Chapter 2, we discussed how to break down essay prompts into their basic components. We mentioned that every essay is asking for <u>causes</u>, <u>reasons</u>, <u>principles</u>, <u>features</u>, <u>similarities</u>, <u>effects</u>, <u>differences</u>, <u>advantages</u>, <u>disadvantages</u> and so on.

Based on that, we can see that this prompt is asking us to identify the <u>biggest social</u> <u>problem</u> facing modern society, and the <u>reasons</u> behind it.

Now that we have identified the core demand of the essay question, let us put down our formal outline. After that, we can write the actual essay, using everything we learned on the Arloo Essay Matrix.

FORMAL OUTLINE

I. INTRODUCTION

    1. Opening statement

    2. Set-up argument

    3. Counterargument

    4. Thesis statement: Poverty trumps health, poor education, crime, drugs and everything else when it comes to social problems because it is the underlying cause of most social problems.

II. BODY

  A. Poverty leads to crime

  B. Poverty leads to poor health care

  C. Poverty leads to poor education

III. CONCLUSION

  A. Summary of supporting arguments

  B. Affirmation of thesis by supporting arguments

ESSAY: *What do you consider to be the single most important societal problem? Why?*

(First Draft. Note: The bold phrases are the **sequential transitions** that help you to write good explanations for your topic sentences. They are very useful in your first draft but you can drop them in your second draft without destroying the logic of your paragraph. The transitional phrase in the last paragraph, "**In conclusion**," may also be dropped to avoid boredom).

In a world reeling under a multitude of social problems, it would seem easy to identify the most important among them. For one thing, health-care provision is so bad that some people get to visit the hospital only in cases of emergency. On the other hand, lack of quality education has been blamed for the huge unemployment figures in the country, with most of the well-paying jobs unfilled because people lack the required training and qualifications. In spite of these issues, poverty can be identified as the single most important societal problem because it is the root cause of most social issues, whether we are dealing with crime, inadequate healthcare, or poor education.

Poverty can be blamed for most of society's problems. And one of these is the problem of crime. **In other words**, poverty creates a situation where people cannot afford to take care of their needs. They cannot get enough food to eat, clothes to wear or a roof over their heads. In such desperate times, people choose the easiest way out. They take to crime and violence purely as a means of survival. Thus, in the big cities with their poverty-ridden ghettos, crime rates are very high. A case in point is

New York City where the crime rate in some poor neighborhoods got so high that the city passed the Stop-and-Frisk Law that enables cops to stop and frisk anybody at all on suspicion of weapons possession without obtaining permission from a judge.

Poverty can also be blamed for the lack of health care in the country. **What is happening is that** health insurance rates in America are very high. A lot of people cannot afford these rates and prefer to buy over-the-counter medications when they fall sick. Others just ignore their health till they are taken to hospital emergency rooms for treatment. The end result is a total absence of health care for millions of Americans. During the debates on the Affordable Health Care Law ("Obamacare"), for example, it came out that over thirty million Americans do not have health care coverage.

Lastly, poverty can be blamed for poor education or lack of it in America. **The point being made is that** in America, children attend schools located in their neighborhood or zip code. Children who live in very poor areas, such as poverty-ridden inner cities, have no choice but to attend the neighborhood school. Most of the time, such schools lack the good teachers, facilities and equipment available to children in well-to-do neighborhoods. This results in poor education, leading to high dropout rates in inner-city schools. For instance, according to dosomething.org, a human rights' advocacy group, 16 to 24-year-old students who come from low income families are seven times more likely to drop out than those from families with higher incomes.

In conclusion, it can be seen that most of the problems of modern society, such as crime, poor education, and inadequate health care, have their roots in poverty. Although some might point to poor government policies and other reasons as the most important societal issues of our time, none of them has the same impact as poverty. This is because, apart from crime, poor education and poor health care, poverty also leads to broken homes, teen pregnancy, juvenile delinquency and a multitude of evils. On this basis, therefore, one cannot be wrong in stating that poverty is the single most important societal problem in society.

(Second Draft)

In a world reeling under a multitude of social problems, it would seem easy to identify the most important among them. For one thing, health-care provision is so bad that some people get to visit the hospital only in cases of emergency. On the other hand, lack of quality education has been blamed for the huge unemployment figures in the country, with most of the well-paying jobs unfilled because people lack the required training and qualifications. In spite of these issues, poverty can be identified as the single most important societal problem because it is the root cause of most social issues, whether we are dealing with crime, inadequate healthcare or poor education.

Poverty can be blamed for most of society's problems. And one of these is the problem of crime. Poverty creates a situation where people cannot afford to take care of their needs. They cannot get enough food to eat, clothes to wear or a roof over their heads. In such desperate times, people choose the easiest way out. They take to crime and violence purely as a means of survival. Thus, in the big cities with their poverty-ridden ghettos, crime rates are very high. A case in point is New York City where the crime rate in some poor neighborhoods got so high that the city passed the Stop-and-Frisk Law that enables cops to stop and frisk anybody at all on suspicion of weapons possession without obtaining permission from a judge.

Poverty can also be blamed for the lack of health care in the country. Health insurance rates in America are very high. A lot of people cannot afford these rates and prefer to buy over-the-counter medications when they fall sick. Others just ignore their health till they are taken to hospital emergency rooms for treatment. The end result is a total absence of health care for millions of Americans. During the debates on the Affordable Health Care Law ("Obamacare"), for example, it came out that over thirty million Americans do not have health care coverage.

Lastly, poverty can be blamed for poor education or lack of it in America. In America, children attend schools located in their neighborhood or zip code. Children who live in very poor areas, such as poverty-ridden inner cities, have no choice but to attend the neighborhood school. Most of the time, such schools lack the good teachers, facilities and equipment available to children in well-to-do neighborhoods. This results in poor education, leading to high dropout rates in inner-city schools. For instance, according to dosomething.org, a human rights' advocacy group, for instance, 16 to 24-year-old students who come from low income families are seven times more likely to drop out than those from families with higher incomes.

It can be seen that most of the problems of modern society, such as crime, poor education, and inadequate health care, have their roots in poverty. Although some might point to poor government policies and other reasons as the most important societal issues of our time, none of them has the same impact as poverty. This is because, apart from crime, poor education and poor health care, poverty also leads to broken homes, teen pregnancy, juvenile delinquency and a multitude of evils. On this basis, therefore, one cannot be wrong in stating that poverty is the single most important societal problem in society

APPENDIX 1

ESSAY # 1: THE OPINION ESSAY
WRITE A PAPER EXPLAINING AND DEFINING ONE OF YOUR CHARACTER TRAITS. INCLUDE WHAT YOU THINK IT MEANS TO HAVE A PARTICULAR TRAIT AND HOW IT AFFECTS OR INFLUENCES CERTAIN AREAS OF YOUR LIFE. EXPLORE YOUR TRAIT'S EFFECTS ON FAMILY, SCHOOL, WORK,
RELATIONSHIPS, COMMUNITY, ETC.

OUTLINE
   I. INTRODUCTION
1. Opening statement: Defining my character trait.
2. Thesis Statement: My dominant character trait, which is persistence, has helped me overcome great odds to enroll in college.
   II. BODY
   A. Positive Effects
1. Family—Role model to younger siblings.
2. School—Not the brightest student but always submitted my work on time.
3. Work—Was retained when others were laid off.
4. Community—Youth volunteer in charge of

clean-ups and fundraising at church.

B. Negative Effects

1. Relationships—Few friends because they complain that I am too stubborn and difficult to work with.

2. Team Sports—Team mates complain that I am the coach's pet and gang up against me.

3. Church—Some people think I am a spy for the church leaders.

III. CONCLUSION

1. Summary of all the various ways my persistence has influenced my life.

2. Reaffirmation of the thesis statement: In spite of the harsh conditions I grew up in, my persistence has helped me to overcome the odds to enroll in college and become a role model to others.

*

Every person can be defined by his or her character traits, whether good or bad. But to describe myself as a person with only good character traits would be a lie. For one thing, I am sometimes mean, unkind, thoughtless and forgetful, and I have done a lot of stupid things in my twenty years in this world. Still, I have also done some things I am very proud of. And one character trait that has helped me is my persistence: I am a person who never gives up when I make up my mind to do something, no matter how difficult or how long it takes.

A character trait refers to certain habits and behaviors of an individual that tell you what type of person he or she is. This makes it possible to predict how such a person is likely to behave in a particular situation. In other words, it gives us a hint into the person's underlying values and beliefs and how he or she lives his life and responds to the world. For example, when we describe a certain person as honest and hardworking or aggressive and lazy, we are describing that person's traits.

My persistence has had a great impact on my life. One of the ways it has influenced my life is that it has helped me to be a role model to my younger siblings. That is to say, being the eldest child, my parents have always taught me to serve as a great example to my siblings. Although I could not read very well in elementary school, I enrolled at the library and brought some books home. It was difficult at first but with a dictionary and some help from my parents I was able to read all the books. This encouraged me to read more. By the time I reached middle school, I was reading the scriptures in church. My siblings were so impressed that they all got books from the library and started reading.

My seven-year-old sister, for example, reads a new book every week.

Secondly, my persistence has influenced my progress in school. The point I am trying to make is that I am not the brightest student in class. But whenever I am given a class assignment, I start work on it the same day. I make sure I get the necessary books and follow the instructions carefully. And I always turn my work in on time. Because of this my teachers always praise me and tell others to follow my example. In my last year in junior high school, for instance, I got an award for always turning my work in before everybody else did.

My persistence has had an impact not only in school but a positive effect on my job as well. The point is that I work in an electronics assembly plant where the work is difficult and complicated. But I make sure I learn every operation till I am perfect at it. And I always do a quality check. Some of my colleagues do not take the trouble to check for quality and are always warned about their attitude. As a result of this, last week there were a lot of lay-offs but I kept my job due to my persistent attitude for quality work. Another instance was when my Line Supervisor praised me on my perfect attendance record during a weekly meeting.

Lastly, my persistence has led to my elevation as the head of the Volunteers Club at my church. The fact is that, every church has lots of activities and events going on at any point in time. I volunteered a lot of my time for these activities. If I did not have the resources or knowledge for an assignment, I made sure that I used every means at my disposal to get the problem solved. After a very difficult Christmas play which I helped to stage, our pastor called me into his office and asked me to set up a Volunteers' Club. At first people did not want to join. But I knocked on their doors and called their telephones so many times that they gave in. Now, we do a lot of things to help our community. For example, every last Saturday of the month, we have a clean-up, clearing weeds and sweeping up trash to beautify the neighborhood.

On the other hand, my persistence has had a few negative effects in my life too. One of these is that I do not have a lot of friends. The point I am making is that whenever I start a project with a friend, I try my best to finish it. But as a result of my persistence, there have been occasions when I have failed to recognize that a plan is not working as well as it should, till it is too late. This leads to a lot of anger and quarrels. As a result, I have few friends. For example, in high school I started a potato garden with a friend on an infertile piece of land. My friend told me about the problem but I insisted on working it and only realized my mistake after we had wasted about two months on the land.

In addition, I find it difficult to take part in team sports like soccer or basketball. That is to say, because of my persistence, I cannot stand it when a teammate is lazy. This is particularly irritating during training since I like to insist on everybody doing their fair share of work. This has led to accusations that I am the coach's pet. A case in point is during one soccer game when one of my teammates refused to run fast enough to tackle an opponent. He ended up scoring and we lost the match. I was not happy about it and we had a big argument. We got suspended for two weeks.

Finally, some of my friends at church think I am a snitch. What happened is that because I am always volunteering for one thing or the other, I spend a lot of time in the Pastor's office. Sometimes, I go there for advice on the details of some of my tasks and responsibilities. Unfortunately, some of my friends think I go there to gossip. As a result, whenever some of my friends at church are having a conversation and they see me, they either change the topic or pretend to be focusing on their books. For instance, one afternoon, I was in the restroom when a couple of them came in. They did not know I was in there and started joking about girls and other things. I overheard one say: "Be careful Eric doesn't hear you say that; he'll report you to Pastor." It hurt my feelings a lot.

In summing up, I will say that my persistence has really made a difference in my life. Although it has sometimes made me lose friends and annoyed some people, it has also helped me to serve as a role model to my siblings, helped me to keep my job, and led to my leadership position in church. But what makes me very proud of this character trait is that, even though I was not the brightest boy in my high school class, I was able to score higher on my college entrance examinations than most of my classmates. And the only reason I was able to do this was because of my persistence.

*

ESSAY # 2: THE ACADEMIC ESSAY **(Note: This essay sample is written in MLA Style)**
IS THE PROBLEM OF DOMESTIC VIOLENCE EXAGGERATED?

OUTLINE
I. INTRODUCTION
  1. Thesis Statement: Far from being exaggerated,

domestic violence is   one of the most devastating
issues of our time because it destroys a lot of
lives.

2. Definition of domestic violence

II. BODY

1. Domestic violence causes physical and
emotional harm and may even lead to loss of
lives.

2. It affects the emotional development of
children.

3. It leads to a waste of state resources used to
treat and rehabilitate victims.

III. CONCLUSION

1. Summary of various arguments

2. Reaffirmation of thesis statement

*

The problem of domestic violence is one of
the most scorching issues of our time. On one hand,
there are those who think it is not such a big deal
since it is as much a part of our lives as teenage
rebellion or midlife crises. Others also think its
effects are exaggerated by the media. But, far from
being an exaggeration, domestic violence can be
described as one of the most devastating social
issues in modern times in view of the level of
destruction it wreaks in society in general, and its

emotional, physical and psychological damage to victims.

Domestic violence usually refers to the "use or threat of physical, sexual or emotional force by spouses, partners, relatives or anyone else with a close relationship with their victims" (Kearns et al. 12). This implies that any act which has a harmful effect on any individual in the family can be described as domestic violence. Such acts include insults, beatings, food deprivations, emotional abuse, forced labor, and so on. It occurs in every sphere of society regardless of education, wealth, race and culture. It is caused by a lot of factors but some of the major ones are cheating, alcoholism, substance abuse, unemployment and poverty.

Domestic violence has caused and continues to create a lot of social problems. But some of the most devastating of these effects are loss of lives and permanent disability sustained by its victims. This implies that the violence between intimate partners and among family members causes a lot of harm and suffering to both victims and perpetrators. Citing studies by Boursnell and Prosser (2010), Lynda Gibbons observes that a lot of domestic attacks involves "slapping, kicking, hitting, punching, burning or scalding, use of weapons or destruction of property; it often results in injury and can lead to death" (12). According to Gibbons, in the UK the Home Office reported that of all the murder cases reported in 2011, 76% of women and 50% of men were killed by people known to the victims (12).

Another effect of domestic violence is the devastating psychological effect it has on children. That is to say, most child victims of domestic violence suffer not only from physical, but also psychological and emotional trauma. DeBoard-Lucas and Grych mention that about 7 million children in the United States live in houses of severe domestic violence (McDonald et al., 2006) in which one parent may beat or burn another, threaten with a weapon, or force them to do things against their will (343). He concludes that children practice what they see going on between parents when they grow up. This is supported by Moylan's findings that children exposed to domestic violence and or child abuse are more likely to show maladaptive behaviors during their teens and beyond (53).

Lastly, domestic violence leads to huge financial losses for the nation. The point is that when domestic violence incidents occur, it involves not only the partners directly concerned but also the law enforcement officers called in, the lawyers handling the disputes and a lot of other things. It also means hospital bills and time lost from work by both abusers and victims. All these add to a huge financial cost to the country, valuable resources which could have been used to provide jobs and services for people. Citing a study by Walby (2004), Gibbons reports that the UK government spends about three billion pounds a year on domestic violence services alone (12).

In conclusion, it can be seen that domestic violence is a problem of huge magnitude since it leads to massive injuries and loss of lives, psychological and emotional trauma in children, and takes a heavy chunk of national resources which could have been put to more productive uses. To describe the problems of domestic violence as an exaggeration, therefore, is to make a mockery of such a tragic issue which affects all mankind.

Works Cited

DeBoard-Lucas, R. L. and Grych, J. H., "Children's Perceptions of Intimate Partner Violence: Causes, Consequences, and Coping," *Journal of Family Violence* (2011) Vol. 26: p343-354. Retrieved from EBSCOhost on August 7, 2013.

Gibbons, Lynda, "Dealing With the Effects of Domestic Violence," *Journal of Emergency Nurse*, Jul 2011 Vol. 19, Issue 4: p12-17. Retrieved from EBSCOhost on August 7, 2013.

Moylan, C; Herrenkohl, T; Sousa, C; Tajima, E; Herrenkohl, R; Russo, M., "The Effects of Child Abuse and Exposure to Domestic Violence on Adolescent Internalizing and Externalizing Behavior Problems," *Journal of Family Violence*. Jan 2010 Vol.25, Issue 1: p53-63. Retrieved from EBSCOhost on August 7, 2013.

Appendix II

ESSAY #1: MY DEEPEST REGRET
OUTLINE:
I. INTRODUCTION
<u>Thesis Statement</u>: I failed to take advantage of an opportunity and I have regretted it since and learned to never procrastinate.
II. BODY
  A. Who? : Some autobiographical details about myself.
  B. When? : The occasion was during my annual vacation when I went to Accra to pick up my check at the office.
  C. Where? : The incident took place in Accra during a visit to my friend's office.
  D. What? : Meeting Billy Ocean
    1. Beginning: Seeing him in the parking lot and failing to recognize him.
    2. Middle: Learning at Eric's office that it was actually Billy Ocean
    3. End: The frantic, fruitless search for Billy Ocean.
III. CONCLUSION

166

E. Why?
    1. Summary of main incidents
    2. Reinforcement/Affirmation of Thesis on
       important lesson learned:
       "Never procrastinate or fail to take
       advantage of an opportunity. When unsure,
       ask for help."

*

Most people, when asked about their deepest regret in life, will tell you they do not have any. For one thing, it is probably the most embarrassing or painful incident in their lives and best forgotten. On the other hand, most people would rather not admit it since it will make you lose respect for them. For me, however, the answer is simple. There is one incident that causes me a lot of pain and regret whenever I think about it. And it is not something I did. Rather, it was something I failed to do and it taught me to never procrastinate.

Billy Ocean is one of the most celebrated musicians in the world. He is a British musician whose peak years were in the late 1980s and the 1990s. He had a lot of hit songs but the most popular were "Caribbean Queen," "Suddenly," "Get out of My Car," "When the Going Gets Tough" and "Stay the Night." In high school, no dance came to life till his song "Caribbean Queen" was played. Indeed, I was so crazy about his music I was nick-named "Billy Ocean."

In July of 2005, I was working as a TV producer at McCann-Eriksson, one of the top advertising agencies in Accra, the capital of Ghana. Because of the noise in the capital, however, I lived in Tema, which was about twenty miles away and much quieter. It had been a hectic year shooting lots of TV commercials so when my vacation time came, I grabbed it with enthusiasm. After a week at home in Tema, I decided to travel to my hometown to have a great reunion with my cousins and uncles. But before leaving, I had to pick up a check from my office. It was with a lot of anticipation that I drove to Accra.

The city was bustling with activity when I arrived. Since it was the peak of the tourism season, a lot of activities were lined up: traditional festivals, theater and street jams. There were long lines of cars, taxis, and trucks caught up in traffic. Impatient drivers tooted their horns at aggressive food vendors and petty traders jostling for space. The few policemen trying to maintain order were ineffective. And everybody was sweating from their efforts. It was mayhem.

I decided to call on Eric, one of my high schoolmates. His office was located in a high-rise along my route. The car park was crowded with lots of smartly-dressed people lounging around. I saw someone who resembled Billy Ocean leaning against one car. I nodded by way of greeting and he responded with a smile and a nod. The resemblance was uncanny but I did not pay any attention to it. What would Billy Ocean be looking for in a small country like Ghana on a weekday? Besides, there had been no news report that he was in town. When I got to my friend's office, he was bubbling over. When he had calmed down a bit, he gave me the reason for his excitement: Billy Ocean had just walked out of his office after signing a deal to perform in Ghana later in the year. Billy Ocean himself! I could have kicked myself till I bled.

I rushed downstairs with Eric so that he would introduce me. But what I actually wanted was a photograph with him. It was a chance of a lifetime! Panting and sweating, we raced into the parking lot. But it was empty. Al the cars—his entourage—had left. The only person in the car park was the security guard who was smiling at an autographed CD in his hand. It was Billy Ocean's "Caribbean Queen"! I asked him where Billy Ocean was. All he told me was "They've left." It almost made me cry.

Eric tried to console me with the fact that I would get to see him in a few months but I would not be comforted. We tried calling Billy's manager to locate him so I could meet and take a photograph with him but no one picked his call. He kept trying till his battery died. I left Eric in the car park but not before extracting a firm promise from him on a ticket to Billy's show. I was beyond heartbroken.

As I drove to my office, I thought about the missed opportunity, an opportunity we had dreamed of since high school. Luckily for Eric, he had fulfilled his. I knew I would probably regret this for the rest of my life. But I had learned my lesson very well. Next time I was in a situation like that where I was not too sure about something, I would go up and ask for clarification. I would never procrastinate again in my life.

You can, therefore, imagine my shock when I got to the office to discover that Billy Ocean and his manager had been to my office to sign the advertizing contract and Billy had taken pictures with everybody in the office. And I mean everybody! When I saw the photographs, it was all I could do not to collapse in pain!

*

ESSAY #2: AN IMPORTANT LESSON I LEARNED

OUTLINE

I. INTRODUCTION

Thesis Statement: If I had not been too quick to dismiss someone due to his scruffy appearance, I would have landed the most lucrative job in my life.

II. BODY

 A. Who? : A few autobiographical details about myself.

 B. When? : The occasion was after graduation from college with my Bachelor's degree and getting an invitation to an interview.

 C. Where? : The visit to the Coca Cola Headquarters.

 D. What? : The interview

   1. Beginning: Preparations for the interview – meeting the scruffy beggar.

   2. Middle: At the interview.

   3. End: The revelation of the board chairman's identity.

III. CONLUSION

    Why?

    1. Summary of main incidents

    2. Reinforcement/affirmation of thesis on important lesson learned:

"Never judge people by their appearance."

*

To say that life is all about the lessons we learn is to make it seem too simple. On one hand, we do not have to read deep meanings into every little incident that takes place in our lives; that would rob us of life's lighter moments. On the other hand, we cannot ignore the lessons that life teaches us to help solve future problems in our lives. Be that as it may, one of the most important lessons I learned in life was that I should never judge people based on their appearance.

My name is Kofi Annan and the last of four children born to my parents. The others are girls. The first born, Amanda, is a doctor at the Teaching Hospital. The next one, Esi, is a successful lawyer and the last girl is Afua, a very successful businesswoman with three shops in London. As you can see, my sisters' successes put an enormous pressure on me to excel in school which I did. And, even though people said I was arrogant, I paid them no mind. After all, why should I lower my standards when it was not my fault I was so smart?

I had just graduated from college with a degree in Business Administration and, after sending out hundreds of applications, I got a letter from the Coca-Cola Company to attend an interview at their headquarters on the 13th of June, 2010. It was the biggest company in my country and, as a child, I used to dream about working there. For one thing, the salary was great and it came with a lot of perks, not to mention the prestige. As I lay in bed the night before the interview, I offered a prayer of thanks to God for the chance to work there. It was an awesome opportunity.

The Coca-Cola Head Office was located at the end of Spintex Road, an area specially set aside for the biggest corporations in Ghana. The buildings were very tall and mostly made of chrome and glass. The tallest among them, almost fifty storeys high, had the Coca-Cola logo embossed on it in huge steel letters. Shady trees lined the car park where well-built uniformed guards strolled about with batons in their belt. It was a really intimidating place.

Just before I entered the building, I was approached by a scruffy-looking man with a tribal mark on his left cheek. He wanted some money for food since he had not eaten for three days. I was already tense because of the interview so I ignored him. When he tried to hold my arm, I shoved him off. He fell into the flower bed. I almost followed up with a kick. Some beggars had no sense of shame.

When I arrived at the conference room, where the interview was being held, I met four other candidates. They appeared more nervous than me but we smiled at each other. Then I was ushered into a smaller office where two distinguished-looking gentlemen interviewed me. I was smart and confident with my answers and one of them commended me on the excellence of my diction. I even managed to get them to laugh a couple of times. It could not have gone better.

As we got to the end of the interview, a door to the side of the office opened and a man in an expensive suit entered, his back facing us as he closed the door. My interviewers rose so I did the same. Then the man turned and faced us, smiling, a tribal mark on his left cheek. I froze—it was the scruffy man I had shoved into the flowerbed! He briefly explained that the incident downstairs was part of the interview process. Since Coca-Cola did a lot of charity work, they were looking for candidates with humanity. Obviously, he added, I had failed in that respect even though I was the smartest candidate. He wished me luck in my job search. Picking up my bag, I left the office, the tears running down my cheeks. What a fool I had been!

When I left the Coca-Cola building, I could not go home. I went to the beach and sat there for a long time, thinking about life and how we live it. I thought about how those to whom much is given must show kindness to the less privileged. I thought about my arrogance and impatience with people I considered inferior. Finally, I decided that from that moment on, I was going to be the kindest person in the world!

WORKS CITED

Arloo, Johnson. "An African under Western Eyes."
bondukusruminations.blogspot.com. 10, Apr.
2012. Web. 26 Oct. 2012.

---. "Gasmilla's 'Aboodatoi' and my daughter's left
foot." *bondukusruminations.blogspot.com.* 17,
Nov. 2012. Web. 30 Oct. 2012.

---. (2009). "The Implications of Positive
Psychology and Wellness for Rehabilitation
Counselor Education."

---. (2009). "The Perils of Generalized Anxiety
Disorder."

---. (2008). "Is Personality Fixed in Childhood?"

---. (2009). "Sexuality and Issues Related to
Sexuality."

DeBoard-Lucas, R. L. & Grych, J. H. (2011).
"Children's Perceptions of Intimate Partner
Violence: Causes, Consequences, and Coping."
Journal of Family Violence Vol 26. 343-354.
Retrieved August 7, 2013, from EBSCOhost.

Foroohar, Rana. (2011). "The Senate's China
Misstep." *Time* 24 Oct. 2011: 17. Print.

Gibbons, Lynda. (2011). "Dealing With the Effects
of Domestic Violence," *Journal of Emergency*

Nurse, Vol 19 (4). 12-17. Retrieved August 7, 2013, from EBSCOhost.

Kirszner, Laurie G., and Stephen R. Mandell. (Eds) (2001). *Patterns for College Writing*. 8th Ed. New York: Bedford/St. Martins.

Lowry, Rich, "Obama vs. the Church," *Time* 20 Feb. 2012: 20. Print.

Mai, Kenneth. "building bridges between your paragraphs."*Harvardwritingcenter.wordpress.com*. 28, Mar. 2013. Web. 16 Aug. 2013.

Mauk, John and John Metz. (2004). *The Composition of Everyday Life: a Guide to Writing*. Boston: Thompson Walworth.

Moylan, C., Herrenkohl, T., Sousa, C., Tajima, E., Herrenkohl, R., & Russo, M. (2010). "The effects of child abuse and exposure to domestic violence on adolescent internalizing and externalizing behavior problems." *Journal of Family Violence*. Vol. 25 (1). 53-63. Retrieved August 7, 2013, from EBSCOhost.

Oz, Mehmet, "Charms of the Quiet Child," *Time* 6 Feb 2012: 40-46. Print.

Quaas, Carole. (2012). "Paper #2 for ENGLISH 1100," English Department, Little Priest Tribal College. Winnebago, Nebraska.

Schuman, Michael, "The Most Important Man in Europe," *Time* 20 Feb. 2012: 28-30. Print.

Walsh, Bryan. (2012). "Rain Forest for Ransom,"
    Time 6 Feb. 2012: 36-39. Print.
"Character." Def. 1. *Webster's New College
    Dictionary*. 3rd ed. 2008. Print.
Wysocki, Ann Frances and Dennis A. Lynch.
    (2009). *The DK Handbook*. Pearson Longman.
Zinsser, William K. (2006). *On Writing Well: The
    Classic Guide to Writing Non-Fiction*. 30th
    Anniv. Ed. HarperCollins.